Acclaim for ADAM PHILLIPS

"A lively treatment of psychoanalysis . . . [which] argues that its goal is the exploration and treatment of disordered—i.e., suppressed—curiosity."
—*The New York Times*

"Roaming from Francis Bacon to Blake, from Melanie Klein to Keats . . . Adam Phillips writes with more grace and wit than we have the right to expect from a Freudian theorist."   —*Elle*

"An extremely lively read . . . Adam Phillips is the latest and brightest of those inventively reinterpreting the subject (of psychoanalysis)."
—*Sunday Telegraph*

"Phillips has virtually invented the essay as a suitable form for penetrating psychoanalytic enquiry."
—Frank Kermode

"Adam Phillips may be the closest thing we have to a philosopher of happiness."   —Adam Mars-Jones

ADAM PHILLIPS

THE BEAST IN THE NURSERY
On Curiosity and Other Appetites

Adam Phillips is the author of *Winnicott; On Kissing, Tickling, and Being Bored; On Flirtation; Terrors and Experts*; and *Monogamy*. Formerly the principal child psychologist at Charing Cross Hospital in London, he lives in England.

THE BEAST IN THE NURSERY

THE BEAST IN THE NURSERY

On Curiosity and Other Thoughts

ADAM PHILLIPS

VINTAGE BOOKS

A Division of Random House, Inc. / New York

A portion of this book originally appeared in somewhat
different form in *London Review of Books*.

Grateful acknowledgment is made to the following for permission to reprint
previously published material: *Faber and Faber Ltd.*: Excerpt from "The Hill of
Intrusion" from *Selected Poems* by W. S. Graham. Reprinted by permission of
Faber and Faber, Ltd., London. *The Free Press* and *Chatto & Windus*: Excerpts from
Narrative of a Child Analysis, volume 4 in *The Writings of Melanie Klein* by Melanie
Klein. Copyright © 1961 by The Melanie Klein Trust. Rights outside the United
States administered on behalf of The Melanie Klein Trust by Chatto & Windus,
London. Reprinted by permission of The Free Press, a division of Simon &
Schuster, and Chatto & Windus, an imprint of Random House UK Ltd. *The Paris
Review*: Excerpt from an interview with Ted Hughes (*The Paris Review* #134,
Spring 1995). Copyright © 1995 by Drue Heinz. Reprinted by permission of
The Paris Review.

The Library of Congress has cataloged the Pantheon edition as follows:
Phillips, Adam.
The beast in the nursery / Adam Phillips.
p.   cm.
Includes bibliographical references.

1. Psychoanalysis. I. Title.
BF 173.P568 1998
150.19'5—dc21

ISBN-13: 978-0-375-70047-7

ISBN-10: 0-375-70047-1

www.randomhouse.com/vintage

Printed in the United States

For Jacqueline Rose

The reason I've begun to speak is that I keep wanting to find out for certain: do other people have such pleasures?

—Fyodor Dostoevsky, *Notes from Underground*

. . . the moral ideal being presented as attractive rather than imperative.

—Henry Sidgwick, *The Methods of Ethics*

Something there badly not wrong.

—Samuel Beckett, *Worstward Ho*

. . . and so everyone according to his cue.

—William Shakespeare, *A Midsummer Night's Dream*,

Act 3, Scene 1

Acknowledgments

Different versions of parts of this book appeared in the *London Review of Books*; *Colère*, edited by Pierre Pachet (Autrement, Paris, 1997); and *Philosophy as Education*, edited by Amelie Rorty (RKP, New York, 1997). I am also grateful to have had the opportunity of presenting earlier versions of "A Stab at Hinting" to various university departments and psychoanalytic groups in Britain and America. These audiences, I hope, will notice their contribution to the final version of this chapter. Presenting consecutive chapters of this book to the Toronto Institute for Contemporary Psychoanalysis made a good deal of difference at a late stage.

Contents

Introduction

All our stories are about what happens to our wishes. About the world as we would like it to be, and the world as it happens to be, irrespective of our wishes and despite our hopes. Our needs thwarted by the needs of others, our romances always threatened by tragedy, our jokes ruined by the people who don't get them. The usual antagonism of daydream and reality. Freud redescribed this old story, at first, as a conflict between what he called the pleasure principle and the reality principle, between the satisfaction we are wanting and whatever frustrates or tempers our desire. And then, rather differently, as a war between the life instinct and the death instinct, a mythic war between nurture, growth, and delight and whatever it is inside us that seeks to destroy our love of life. Freud was not, of course, the first person to notice how precarious our love of life is, how vulnerable this love is the older we get. But he was excessively preoccupied by what interfered with the destiny of this particular passion, a passion that seemed at once fundamental and more vividly imagined through its failure than its success. It was through symptoms, paradoxically, that Freud got a glimpse of what sexuality might be; through slips of the tongue the plenitude of the unspoken revealed itself. And as a very late Romantic, Freud found the passions and perplexities of the child exemplary; the child with her consuming interests, her inexhaustible questions, and her insisting body. The child who is learning to make mistakes, figuring out how to become a person, through the curious combinations of word and gesture, and the gaps between them.

Freud, in fact, translated back to very early childhood the traditional story of growing up as a process of disillusionment. He described a minor epic—a kind of ironic quest romance—going on inside the child's mind. The child was imagined as wanting something essential (feeling hungry) and then, in its absence omnipotently fantasizing the longed-for breast. Since the breast was unlikely to appear the moment it was desired, it could nevertheless be imagined instantaneously, according to the child's wish. This was the pleasure principle in action. But then, of course, the child begins to notice that beyond a certain point the imagined breast is not sufficiently nourishing, and in actuality, not nourishing at all. So the reality principle involves the child's learning to defer gratification, acknowledging his desire as an obstacle course, because his desire entails something other than himself. Ultimately, the child needs to abrogate his omnipotence—abjure his magic—and learn to wait. Accepting his dependence, and bearing the fact of his parents' independence of him, he makes good his survival and his pleasure by relinquishing his fantasies of self-sufficiency (his omnipotent self-satisfyings). There are perils to this process—who the child and his parents happen to be, the transgenerational history the child crawls into—but it is a necessary disillusionment. Being realistic is a better guarantee of pleasure; it is an injunction to want sensibly. The child may expect the earth of himself and others, but if he grows up properly, he will begin to want something else. But what happens to wanting when it isn't wanting everything, and when it isn't wanting what one wants? Or, to put it another way—from an adult point of view, as it were—how do we decide what a good story about wanting is? And which stories will sustain our appetite, which is, by definition, our appetite for life? Even to want death you have to be alive. Morality is the way we set limits to wanting; the way we redescribe desiring so that it seems to work for us.

Kleinian psychoanalysts have been among the most lucid exponents of the dangers of what Freud called omnipotence,[1] of all the ways a person can attack or refuse his need for other people, of how the fantastic refuges from need are forms of emotional starvation—megalomanias and distortions of reality born of fear. "When omnipotent fantasy dominates," Hanna Segal writes, "the desired state of affairs in accordance with the pleasure principle predominates over the realistic. Reality testing has failed . . ."; and the consequence of such fantasy, she is quite clear, is "misperception." The child—or the adult in this all-too-available state of mind—sees what he wants, not what is there. There is an obvious question here about who decides, or what the criteria might be for, what is considered an accurate perception. Indeed, this is also a version of development—of acculturation—as punishment. That is to say, this kind of realism always has gravity but not gusto (like most Kleinian and orthodox Freudian writing); but a kitsch seriousness too easily becomes the order of the day. In this story, from the child's point of view the world made by wanting is the world; from the adult's point of view the child—suffering from the delinquency of misperception—is either not quite right, or wrong. There is something essential the child has failed to comply with, to observe.

There is a dilemma here that cannot be resolved merely by taking sides. Desire without something that resists it is insufficient, wishy-washy, literally immaterial; it meets with nothing—nothing but itself— if it is too exactly met (as in omnipotent fantasy). But a world that too much resists my desire is uninhabitable, unlivable. I can only make it my own—find myself in it—through my wanting something from it. Thinking about a meal won't make me full; but neither will eating a meal I have no appetite for. Only my hunger turns the food into a meal. So we should give two cheers for what psychoanalysts call "omnipotence," because it is a version of what Blake called "vision." And vision, in Blake's sometimes (and perhaps inevitably) weird sense of the word, is the necessary complement—or counterargument, as nuance—to the very real misgivings of the analysts. Humankind *can* bare too much reality; sensible wanting, intelligible wanting, can also be the death of desire. As Freud knew, compliance and appetite are always uneasy bedfellows. And appetite is another word for imagination. "Nearly all of us have felt," Northrop Frye wrote in his great commentary on Blake,

> at least in childhood, that if we imagine that a thing is so, it therefore either is so or can be made to become so. All of us have to learn that this almost never happens, or happens only in very limited ways; but the visionary, like the child, continues to believe that it always ought to happen. We are so possessed with the idea of the duty of acceptance that we are inclined to forget our mental birthright, and prudent and sensible people encourage us in this. That is why Blake is so full of aphorisms like "If the fool would persist in his folly he would become wise." Such wisdom is based on the fact that imagination creates reality, and as desire is a part of imagination, the world we desire is more real than the world we passively accept.

It cannot, of course, even in the terms of its own argument, be a "fact" that imagination creates reality. But it can be a useful wish, a fiction of prolific consequences. Certainly, desire and passive acceptance seem unpromising as alternatives, though for Blake—and in psychoanalysis for Freud, Ferenczi,

Winnicott, Milner, and Searles—they were pro-
ductive antagonists (or "contraries," in Blake's language). By concentrating too scrupulously on what
wishing disavows, analysts have denied what wishing
affirms. The child, after all, is making a promising
world for herself. The visionary, or the child, or infantile sexuality, or the dream, or the joke, or the unconscious itself, are all, among many other things,
figures for an alternative to passive acceptance, for
the possibility of remaking, for revision as a way of
protecting our pleasures.

What Blake called vision Freud redescribed as
dreamwork when we are asleep and erotic life when
we are (more or less) awake. To "have" an unconscious is to have work going on behind the scenes, to
be subject to what André Green calls "kinds or
forms of reasoning which lead us astray." These
stranger ways of thinking that inhabit us are like the
unofficial (or illicit) work we do on our experience.
Revealing the idiosyncrasy of our desire—or what in
different languages might be called our madness, or
our passion, or our imagination—the odd sense we
can make of things is both a consummate gift and an
ironic competence (no one could be better at living
your life than you). These other ways of thinking
that lead us astray have their own disruptive vitality,

though we often experience our exuberance as dismay, our leases of new life as dread. There is, in other words, a way of describing our inner anomalies as signs of life, and no less terrifying for being so. We may know what is on our minds, but not what is on the other minds inside us. In this sense we are as separate from ourselves as from other people.

This capacity for transformation, for the imaginative and often bizarre refashioning of everyday experience, was originally the child's unerring, ineluctable talent for making something of his own from whatever he finds (the given is inert until it becomes the made). Revision with a view to satisfaction is the child's project (and so psychoanalysis asks, by the same token, what resists revision, what will redescription not change?). Children are fervent in their looking forward to things, whereas adults can lose a sense of what is there for the taking. The child, it seemed to Freud, was the virtuoso of desire, for whom the meaning of life could only be its satisfactions. And yet it was this appetite—the individual's lifeline—that seemed most under threat from within and from without: from the death instinct, and from what Freud referred to rather abstractly as culture. Psychoanalysis, in other words, was about what

killed people's appetite, about how we are most in-
timidated by the only thing that can sustain us. So it
was to the fate of interest—of that imaginative
hunger called curiosity, which is part of what I'm
calling the love of life—in each person's life that
Freud turned his attention. Having things to look
forward to, making things to look forward to, he realized, can become a lost art. To forget the pleasures
of anticipation is to forget memory itself.

If we are to go on making and taking our pleasure, Freud implies, there are three things we have to
be able to do: involve other people, make good our
losses, and enjoy (or at least tolerate) conflict. This is
the imaginative resilience, the ruthlessness we must
foster, or our spirits will flag. It is, perhaps, one of the
more rueful ironies of the psychoanalytic vision, that
pleasure should seem such a tall order, that to secure
it we have to meet such stringent (moral) demands.
Indeed, what Freud maps out is the complicated relationship between our struggle for pleasures and
our struggle for survival. It is, of course, nonsense
from a Darwinian point of view, and logical from a
Freudian point of view, that they could be at odds
with each other (there are laws of nature but not
laws of happiness). And yet, if one of the virtues of

psychoanalysis is that by speaking up for conflict it allows people sufficient complexity, one of its complementary vices is a certain blind spot—an unwillingness to sponsor people's potential for ease (things are only difficult if you can't do them). Amusement is there if you want it. It is one of the most striking things about children that, in their play, good things can come easily.

Psychoanalysis is about what stops good things coming easily, about how we have to acknowledge, but also how we seem to need to create, accurate obstacles to satisfaction. It is a story about fluency and its interruption. About what people are inspired by, and how this can turn into a feeling of being driven. It is the supposition of this book that inspiration is the best word we have for appetite, and that appetite is the best thing we have going for us (children are visionaries simply in their commitment to first things first). It is appetite that makes things edible, just as it is imagination that makes lives livable once they are economically viable. And, as children take for granted, lives are only livable if they give pleasure: that is, if we can renew our pleasures, remember their intensities. And so be delighted by hope, not merely persecuted or protected by it.

part one

THE INTERESTED PARTY

I can swim like the others only I have a better memory than the others. I have not forgotten my former inability to swim. But since I have not forgotten it my ability to swim is of no avail and I cannot swim after all.

—KAFKA, *Parables and Paradoxes*

I

When H. G. Wells accused Henry James in a letter of having sacrificed his life to art, James replied with characteristically artful indignation: "I live, live intensely, and am fed by life, and my value, whatever it might be, is my own kind of expression of that. Art makes life, makes interest, makes importance." James's value, he asserts, is in his expression of what he is fed by. Something called life, lived intensely, feeds him; and he makes something of it, something of his own, called art.

What he is describing is both the gift of the artist and the necessity of the so-called ordinary person. We cannot help but transform our experience—Freud's emblem for this is dreamwork—and we cannot help but express ourselves. Whether we like it or not, we are making something of what we are given, even when we are merely making do. People come for psychoanalysis when they are feeling undernourished, and this is because—depending on one's psychoanalytic preferences—either what they have been given wasn't good enough, so they couldn't do enough with it, or because there is something wrong with their capacity for transformation. In James's terms, they are the failed artists of their own lives. They have been unable for whatever reason to make something sufficiently sustaining out of what was supposed to nourish them. They cannot make interest; the kind of interest James intimates that might make one love life; or feel nourished by whatever it was that one happened to be given. And in the light of this there are, one could say, two kinds of psychoanalysis, or rather, psychoanalysis comes under two kinds of description. One kind of psychoanalysis aims to make good—if only by reconstruction of the early environmental provision—an environmental deficit. At its most extreme—or by its critics—this is called analysis as a corrective emotional experience. The other kind of psychoanalysis aims to restore the artist in the patient, the part of the person that makes interest despite, or whatever, the early environment. At its most extreme, for the artist of her own life, it is not so much a question of what she has been given but of what she can make of what she has been given (no one chooses their parents, but everyone invents them, makes what they can of them). The psychoanalytic model here is the dream, or the child's infantile sexual theory, in which so-called reality functions more like a hint than an instruction, setting the dreamer and the child off on the work of transformation.

When James writes in his charged self-defense to Wells, "My value, whatever it might be, is my own kind of expression. . . . Art makes life, makes interest, makes importance," he is both privileging this notion of self-expression—the idiosyncratic privacy of transformation—and regarding it as inextricable from, of a piece with, living intensely. For James, life was not sacrificed to art, nor was art an alternative to life; they were integral to each other. It would be like saying of someone that he sacrificed his life to dreaming by going around in the day looking for day residues to use.

So by the same token, the artist in James is not divorced from what we might call the materialist. James's sophisticated subtlety always invites us to note the crudely literal; in actuality it is sex that makes life (James had no children); and for James his art did give him importance—the power of a place—in the highly competitive turn-of-the-century market for novels. And, of course, in the pun of my title, the interest that art made for him was also the financial return on his investment (to be interested in something or someone is a gamble with uncertain returns). Art makes interest; it is a way of investing something that might be called life or experience, that is a species of risk. Interest may or may not accrue, but art, James intimates, is a version of stocks and shares; the market fluctuates. Something is transformed—work is done on it—in the service of making interest, sustaining curiosity, keeping one's appetite alive. If James's novels don't make interest in the readers come alive, they won't read on, they won't buy them. The writer's appetite has to incite the readers' appetite.

Psychoanalytic theory—in all of its various versions—is a set of stories about this process of transformation that James calls Art (with a capital *A*) and we can call the art of everyday life; it is a set of stories about how we can nourish ourselves to keep faith with our belief in nourishment, our desire for desire. What every patient tells the analyst, one way and another, is that the appetite (and care) that kept them going at the very beginning ineluctably complicated into both the source and the saboteur of their confidence. What we now call desire is both hope and the impossibility of hope: that the life in us is not always on our side. So how do we become sufficiently interested in our lives to want to go on living them if, as James believes, interest is something we make? And despite the fact that, at least in ordinary language, the opposite of making interest is losing it, not finding it.

Ordinary language assumes, in other words—as did Freud, at least in his earlier work—that interest is something we've already got. We start, as it were, from a position of interest (indeed, all our ways of pathologizing people are descriptions of their losing interest in the appropriate things, or rather, ideals). So I want to consider in what sense or under what conditions interest is made, and how we manage, or plot, to lose it. And I want to suggest that the fact that we are interested at all—and our preconditions for being interested—are every bit as telling as what we happen to be interested in. (If we want to read about the cost, or the sheer implausibility of interest, we have to read, say, Beckett, or Frances Tustin on autism, or W. R. Bion on attacks on linking, or Freud and Klein on the death instinct, or Ernest Jones on aphinisis.) It is both ordinary, in the best sense, and wishful, in the best sense, to take interest for granted. Every depression, every act of psychic deadening, bears witness to the risk of interest and curiosity. "Whatever excites and stimulates our interest is real," James's brother William wrote in his *Principles of Psychology,* knowing how much we can fear the real.

Psychoanalysis is the art of making interest out of interest that is stuck. We don't, in other words, believe that the football fan isn't really interested in football; we believe that he is far more interested in football than he can let himself know. In psychoanalysis we treat the objects of interest as clues and cues, as commas that look like periods. Every object of desire is an obscure object of desire; leading us to ask both, why this rather than that, and why anything at all? Free-floating attention itself, as a method, is a tribute to the vagaries of interest. Evenly hovering attention wants to land. In other words, there is, as Freud implies, a will to interest that can usurp a capacity for it.

Indeed, to talk about the unconscious is to refer to the fact that we are interested in things despite ourselves; we have more or less conscious preferences or affinities, but we find ourselves living out alternative, often puzzling, interests. I go to meet a friend, but I find myself doing some shopping on the way; I fall in love with a woman, but she reminds me of my father. Like sunflowers whose suns are various and hidden, we see ourselves going in all sorts of directions, often at once. This is what psychoanalysis formalizes for the patient: a repertoire of personal tropisms, of the idiosyncratic drifts of attention called unconscious desire. In psychoanalysis we track the way the patient makes and breaks interest for himself. And we implicitly or explicitly persuade him that some interests are better than others. That, say, it's better to spend one's time looking at art rather than exclusively at bodies; or that conversation and relationship is better than inner delirium; or that the sense that nothing connects with nothing is dispiriting rather than cheering. Every analyst will have their own—mostly unconscious—repertoire of suitable interests for a good person. This seems to me (as luck would have it) both inevitable and desirable; as integral to the process of doing analysis, which involves, by definition, a clash and a company of interests. But it is worth wondering, from a psychoanalytic point of view, what we are doing when we are interested in something or someone; what our preconditions for interest are and how they work. Both how the patient got to be interested, and how she got to be interested in *this* (person, activity, film). It is a question of the relationship—that is at the heart of erotic life—between incitement and excitement. If we are lucky, or when we feel alive or sufficiently awake, something is always getting us going, apparently making us a promise. We are always more promised than promising because we are so ingenious at resisting the lead of our desire. Defensiveness is a talent for willfully reading clues, for not paying sufficient attention to our attention; for preferring safety to whatever else is around.

II

One of the first words in psychoanalysis for what I am calling interest was curiosity. For Freud infantile sexuality was a kind of apotheosis of curiosity; it was both its origin for the individual and the paradigm for all its later forms. In Freud's descriptions in the early works—pre 1910—it is almost as though the child is lived by, or lives through, her sexual curiosity; what Strachey translates as the sexual researches of children. The index of the Standard Edition has more references under the heading "Sexual researches of children" than under any of the other sexual subjects. What united, in Freud's view, the artist, the scientist, the lawyer, the teacher, was that they were all interested, in however disguised a form, in the sexual questions of childhood. Psychoanalysis was distinguished by being curious about curiosity, about its provenance and function in a person's life. The child's profundity, in Freud's view, was in the quality of its curiosity. When he refers to children who have been told the facts of life but go on believing their own sexual theories, who "go on worshipping their own idols in secret," he is paying tribute to the child as someone unseduced by reality, unimpressed by other people's truths. The relentlessness of the child's questions, the sense that the child's curiosity was his destiny—this was what Freud took to heart. The child knew what he was interested in—where babies come from, the difference between the sexes, his parents' relationship—these were the child's inspiration. They weren't options—the child was not casting around for a hobby, or in some supermarket, spoiled for choice—they were urgencies. And what the child's curiosity highlighted was the child's need to know and the impossibility of his being satisfied. As a kind of parody of theoretical or epistemological man, the Freudian child is driven by questions and doesn't believe any of the answers, except his own that he finds satisfying (for the child, meaning is the polite word, the sophisticated word for pleasure). He is addicted to, driven by, what he doesn't know. But his well-being, if not his actual future, depended on what Freud called his sexual researches, the making up his theories. The child's sexual life was his theory-making. The child lived intensely his sensual life, out of which he made his necessary art. And the implications of this for psychoanalysis itself—and for education—were intriguing: Freud implicitly identifying with the curious child, but also the picture of the analyst and his patient—or the teacher and her student—as two children exchanging their sexual theories. In *On the Sexual Theories of Children,* Freud explicitly likens the child's fantastic sexual speculations to the theories of the adult. "These false sexual theories," Freud writes,

have one very curious characteristic. Although they go astray in a grotesque fashion, yet each one of them contains a fragment of real truth; and in this they are analogous to the attempts of adults, which are looked at as strokes of genius, at solving the problems of the universe which are too hard for human comprehension.

Freud gives us a theory of theorizing that puts all theory, including his own, into question. The origins of the child's theories, he writes, "are the components of the sexual instincts which are already stir-

ring in the childish organism." The child is not exactly what we might call an empiricist; he simply
uses so-called real things as food for thought, as what
Henry James calls in his *Notebooks* "germs" for stories.
What we might think of as the elaborate coherence
of a theory Freud refers to as "going astray in a
grotesque fashion." Knowledge for the child, as for
the adult, is a sexually inspired project; just like the
dreamwork, out of a fragment of truth, of something real like a day residue, peculiar personal truths
are woven out of unconscious desire. In Freud's scenario the "fragment of truth" in the child's own theory comes from the biological facts of life (the facts
of life are true in so far as one wants to have or avoid
having a baby; if reproduction was not the project,
or the purpose, what then would correspond to the
fragment of truth?). Once Freud positions himself as
the one who can identify the fragment of truth in the
child's theory, he can differentiate himself from
the child. He has to find a position from which the
child's position also looks naive, absurd, or merely
wrong. If no one's theory can be made to look
ridiculous, how are we going to tell our theories
apart? (The notion of truth in this context makes humiliation both possible and necessary.) There are

fragments of truth and the going astray in a grotesque fashion. This is the difference Freud both equivocates about and wants us to keep in mind.

All curiosity in Freud's view "re-awakens the traces, which have since become unconscious, of his first period of sexual interest." And these traces are traces of both knowledge and method. Both what the child made (made up), and how he went about making it. Our own ways of being interested link us to the past. We have acquired official and unofficial habits of inquiry (and so we have an official and un-official personal development). Our preconditions for loving are bound up with, are informed by, this first period of sexual interest.

What is clear in Freud's account of children's sex-ual curiosity is that it was akin to, or a form of, ap-petite; it had to be satisfied, but by a fantasy, a story, as though the child's instinctual life partly took the form of a hunger for coherent narrative, for satisfy-ing fiction. Often stimulated, as Freud frequently points out, by the birth of a sibling—and other peo-ple, of course, were beginning to participate in Freud's psychoanalysis as both colleagues and ri-vals—these fantasies, whether they be sexual theo-ries or the more disguised and sophisticated family romances, were the medium for the child's struggle for psychic survival, the child's attempts, however forlorn, to refind a place in the world. Theory, Freud intimates, is intrinsically rivalrous; it is about being better placed than someone else. The child's curiosity and theory-making was, in a real sense, about how he came to be there, and in what sense he was still there after the birth of the sibling. And this means, of course, that in a sense he is not still there; he has been displaced. He is elsewhere. Wishing is the sign of loss; wanting things to be otherwise because they are not as they are supposed to be. For the child to live his curiosity is itself an acknowledgment of loss, of wanting as the sign of life.

And yet despite our hunger for elegiac knowledge—for knowledge as elegy, as being about what we have lost—the child's discoveries in Freud's equivocal account are not quite or always as reassuringly painful as the by now familiar post-Freudian talk of lack, disillusionment, and mourning might suggest. Psychoanalytic theory has become obsessed by, indeed obsessional about, loss, but for Freud there is also an imaginative plenitude, a manifest exhilaration about the ways in which children go astray in a grotesque fashion. It is the child's always paradoxical resilience—the inventions born of apparent insufficiency, the refusal of common sense, of the facts of life—that Freud is taken by. But it has been Freud's version of the child's formative helplessness that has been taken up in different ways by Lacan, Winnicott, and Klein. For each of them the child is someone for whom something essential is missing, or lost, or destroyed: the unified image in the mirror, the potential wealth and solace of the mother, the father's entitlement, the parents' sexual relationship; whichever way it is construed, the child is essentially the maker of individious comparisons. As though the child's strongest wish or deepest desire is to grow up, to become more sexually or intellectually competent, to not be a child. As though the child experiences himself as exclusively inferior to the adult (in certain versions of romanticism, of course, the adult is seen as a diminished child). In other words, a potentially nonlinear theory is underpinned by a simple linear progress myth. What children supposedly suffer from is not being what they think of as adults; and adulthood becomes the afterlife for children, which means a growing acquaintance with the unappeasable nature of desire. You can become an adult who is supposed to know, or a child with endless questions. Whether or not we try to escape from our question marks, psychoanalysts are committed to the idea of a life as somehow organized around, in rela-

tionship to, absence. We are the animals for whom
something is missing and for whom what is missing is
always privileged. What is absent, ironically, is what
is there for us to be interested in. Our curiosity depends upon a receding horizon. Good stories of
profit and loss are indeed bewitching. And yet when
we describe children, or adults, as insufficient, we
might wonder, insufficient compared to what? Why,
for example, hasn't the death of God been the death
of our preoccupation with ourselves as lacking?
Making a fetish of absence is the last move in a
worn-out theology. Our fantasies of plenitude can
be unconscious forms of self-mockery—ways of humiliating ourselves—and it is in the child that these
preoccupations often get located. The theoretical
vogue for lack and insufficiency has become a perverse boast: a way of disqualifying the child's very
real imaginative achievements. As though the child is
somehow cursed by what he doesn't have, by what's
missing (competence, sexual maturity, independence,
and so on). The child—unlike the adult—is not
merely compensating for not being an adult, or for
not being self-sufficient, because there is no purpose
in the child's life other than living it. In other words,
it is not the child who believes in something called
development.

If there is a vividly frustrated child at the heart of psychoanalysis—a child who has stolen the show with his anguish, a child whose abject resourcelessness is somehow exemplary—there is another Freudian child who has been mislaid. This child is not merely the satisfied child (though he is alluded to, I think, in contemporary accounts of the amazingly competent and accomplished infant of empirically based developmental theory, the child who is a natural at the double act of infancy). The child I am referring to, that psychoanalysis has mislaid—who is rarely the subject of psychoanalytic theory—is the child with an astonishing capacity for pleasure, and indeed the pleasures of interest, with an unwilled relish for sensuous experience which often unsettles the adults, who like to call it affection. This child who can be deranged by hope and anticipation—by ice cream—seems to have a passionate love of life, a curiosity about life, which for some reason isn't always easy to sustain. Of course, the ordinary childhood experience of delight that I am describing has elements of omnipotence in it, but to call it merely omnipotence is to overload the dice. I would prefer to call it a kind of ecstasy of opportunity (Blake called it exuberance).

But whatever it is, this childhood relish does not fit easily into the ordeal of psychoanalytic development. Because it is easy to sentimentalize, and to idealize, the visionary qualities of the child, this part of the legacy of Romanticism—that is, in Blake and Wordsworth and Coleridge most explicitly—has been abrogated by psychoanalysis. Freud's child as sexual theorist, "astray in a grotesque fashion," is a version of the visionary poet of Romanticism, who is of course neither innocent nor in any sense conflict-free. Or to put it more straightforwardly, children say some very strange things. They seem to care a lot about what is going on. And they are very interested in bodies. They really want to learn what goes in and out of them, and what goes on inside them.

Unfortunately, the child described by psychoanalysis usually has only two genres available to him: romantic comedy or tragedy. In tragedy his curiosity ennobles the hero and kills him; in the comic romance his curiosity makes a mockery of him. It is the fate of what I am calling interest, in these genres, that it either invites agony and posthumous fame, or mild but enchanting humiliation. The child as Oedipus or the child as Don Quixote. And yet in his great paper " 'Civilized' Sexual Morality and Modern Nervous Illness," Freud suggests, in his description of infantile sexuality, a quite different destiny for the child's curiosity. Or rather he suggests that the fact that the child knows exactly what interests her—that is, sexuality—makes curiosity itself a scandal for culture; and partly because it is an infinite pleasure for the child. The child, that is to say, inevitably sublimates;[2] she makes up theories, in fantasy and language, but they are about nothing but sexuality (about what goes in and out of bodies and what goes on inside them). A kind of sublimation that is always refusing to play the game, that keeps, as it were, pointing at bodies, and what they might do for pleasure. Sublimation, in other words, is a figure for remaking, for redescription, but in the service of delight. So the question for the child (and then the adult) becomes: what can I turn sex into and still get sufficient satisfaction, still find these things—reading, getting rich, failing—worth looking forward to and actually doing?

Freud believed, Philip Rieff wrote in *The Triumph of the Therapeutic*, that psychoanalysis could not make people happy, but it could make them less miserable. And yet in Freud's description of the child, the child represents the refusal of stoicism—sublimation as an intimation of its own limits: words to get us back to bodies.

III

In " 'Civilized' Sexual Morality and Modern Nervous Illness" Freud makes a simple and still astonishing assertion: "the sexual behaviour of a human being often lays down the pattern for all his other modes of reacting to life." Integral to, indeed constitutive of, the sexual behavior of children is their curiosity about sex. One could almost say that their curiosity *is* their sexuality. And yet it is their very curiosity about sex, Freud suggests, that creates for them a fundamental conflict with what he calls the "ideals of education." Children want to know about sexuality, but the grown-ups tell them they need to know about something else; and they need to know about something else—call it culture—to distract them from what they are really interested in. Education, Freud implies, teaches the child either to lose interest in what matters most to her or to compromise that interest. Interest has to have something added to it, called education, to make it acceptable. Freud goes on to describe the debilitating effect of what is referred to in quotation marks as "civilized" sexual morality. "In general," Freud writes,

> I have not gained the impression that sexual abstinence helps to bring about energetic and self-reliant men of action, or original thinkers or bold emancipators and reformers. Far more often it goes to produce well-behaved weaklings who later become lost in the great mass of people that tend to follow, unwillingly, the leads given by strong individuals.

Sounding rather like Reich here, Freud is quite clear that civilized sexual morality, with its injunction to abstinence, ironically undermines all the culture's most cherished character ideals (he may also be wondering, of course, what it is about psychoanalysis that might make people want to follow him).

Indeed, if we read this paper (which, interestingly, makes no reference to the Oedipus complex) prospectively, we could think of what Freud calls here civilized sexual morality, or the ideals of education, as forerunners of the death instinct—that it is the function of culture to kill curiosity; or to do that subtler diverting or distracting or dispatching of curiosity—which Freud does refer to in this paper—

called sublimation. Through sublimation—as a psychoanalytic concept notably recalcitrant to elaboration—we can have it both ways. Or at least, that's what we need to believe: that's what we hope. "We may well raise the question," Freud concludes his paper somberly,

> whether our "civilised" sexual morality is worth the sacrifice which it imposes on us, especially if we are still so much enslaved to hedonism as to include among the aims of our cultural development a certain amount of satisfaction of individual happiness.

Why, Freud seems to be asking, have we bothered to include among our ideals a bit of satisfaction for the individual? Why haven't we dispensed with individual satisfaction altogether? Why not after childhood just lose interest in happiness?

There is a simple, and to some people an obviously simplistic, logic here. Children, Freud suggests, are hedonists—preoccupied with the erotics of pleasure. "The sexual behaviour of a human being often lays down the pattern for all his other modes of reacting to life." Civilization wants to foreclose the child's real interest. Education—rather like much

developmental theory—offers the child a new religion: the religion of substitution. Symbol formation,
transitional phenomena, the law of the father, the
Oedipus complex, the sharable sublimations of
art—the message to the child is the same: there is no
substitute, but you must find one; you must give
something up with no guarantee that what you will
get in its place will even be sufficient, let alone as
good or better.

You must lose interest in order to find it; this is the
gospel of development. You must mourn your hopeless passion for your parents, your imaginary, idealized identifications, your absorbing sensuality; you
must acquire language. How can we possibly imagine development—or indeed a viable life—without
the idea of substitution? And yet this is exactly what
Freud is asking us to do in " 'Civilized' Sexual
Morality and Modern Nervous Illness." We are, he
says, by nature interested, indeed fascinated, by sexuality, and then civilization invites us to *remake* our
interest, to fashion ourselves into educable creatures.
The cost of losing interest in what interests us is, he
writes, "an increase of anxiety about life and of fear
of death," and a proneness to strong leaders; as
though, by implication, democracy is only for those
who can bear their sexual aliveness. In other words,

we are radically imperiled by our gospel of substitution: our willingness to be initiated into abstinence, the psychoanalytic term for substitution.

We may not know what sublimation is, but we all get a bit agitated, or suspicious, if someone suggests, as Freud does here, that it may not be such a good thing. (Donald Kaplan begins his appropriately entitled essay "What Is Sublimated in Sublimation" with the words "The whole idea of sublimation has been a vagrant problem for psychoanalysis from the very beginning." As Kaplan acknowledges, sublimation—as the way we redirect our sexual desire—is essentially a problem of vagrancy and beginnings, of translation as nomadic.) We prefer the barbarity of culture to the barbarity of nature, even though we usually can't tell them apart; there is nothing more cultural than our fantasies about nature. No one can be pastoral about sex now, and to talk of an uncultured sexuality is a contradiction in terms. In a certain sense, there is no sexuality without culture (all art may be sublimated sexuality, but then so is all sexuality). And yet in this paper—written when Freud was in his early fifties, and Freud was no born-again adolescent by nature—Freud offers us his instructive romance, so much against the grain of most of his own writing and that of the psychoanalysts who were to follow him. "In man," Freud writes, "the sexual instinct does not organically serve the purposes of reproduction at all, but has as its aim the gaining of particular kinds of pleasure." This was the real scandal of what Freud called infantile sexuality. Not only that it is a (thwarted) warm-up for adult life—and therefore that children are prototypically sexual creatures—but that infantile sexuality, with its sole aim of "gaining particular kinds of pleasure," is the fundamental paradigm for erotic life. The counter-Darwinian implications of a human sexuality untied to procreation—or even antireproductive—are shocking. It may not be that children can't wait to grow up and have proper reproductive sex—a comforting belief for the adults—but that, in Freud's view, children have discovered, through their immature sexual constitutions, one truth about sex: that it is about the giving and getting of certain pleasures, and that civilized notions of relationship and family merely obscure this. Sex, for children in this unlikely Freudian pastoral, issues in nothing but sensual delight, in appetite regained.

"Sublimation," Hans Loewald begins his great book on the subject, "to the psychoanalyst, is at once privileged and suspect." As, one might add, it is for the child (people's first sentences about sublimation are always telling; the question, after all, is, how and why does it start?). The child is not merely a tragic or comic hero; he is an ecstatic, an aesthete involved in an absurd project of sublimating in order to diminish the necessity of sublimating; someone who believes, in Loewald's sublimated abstract language of theory, that

> differentiated or "further advanced" modes of psychic life [are] defensive, even illusory in nature, concealments or more or less intriguing, fanciful embellishments of the elementary, the psychic reality of instinctual-unconscious life.

The child, in other words, is not fooled by the so-called advantages of development, and what they obscure. But of course, to try and describe an unsublimated life would itself be a consummate act of sublimation. There is an irony built into theorizing about sexuality. But Freud's story in his paper " 'Civilized' Sexual Morality and Modern Nervous Illness" confronts us rather starkly—almost as a kind of parable—with a more immediate, less abstract question: how do we—or can we ever—tell the difference between what we are interested in and what we should be interested in?

The child in Freud's story represents an unwilled inevitable momentum of curiosity, what I would want to call a capacity for absorption or affinity, a willingness to be lost in something or someone. What Freud calls civilized morality, the ideals of education, in this paper, I would redescribe in Winnicottian terms as compliance; that which I do because not doing it is too dangerous.

How do we know the child is interested in sex, Freud wonders? Because he or she, at certain times, is endlessly asking questions about it, and secretly making up stories about it that Freud pointedly wants to call theories; formulating, in fantasy, unconscious wishes. The child's interest is in the stories (what James referred to as making interest through art). Language is the child's best way of being this curious, keen, theory-bound hedonist. And like all serious hedonists—and it is of course the problem with hedonists that they are always serious—the child is not a crude literalist. He is not a pornographer; he is committed to the erotics of subtler mediation, of doing sex partly with words. But he won't settle for a diet of words only (what

Freud calls abstinence). Words are his route back to bodies.

All psychoanalytic theory celebrates and encourages the child's developing ability to extend the range of his interests beyond his body and the bodies of his parents in relation to each other. Indeed, what else could it propose? The child must acquire, at least officially, a rather more occasional interest in his and other people's bodies, and a spellbound commitment, through education, to the language and character ideals of his culture. And yet Freud implies in this paper that the inevitable and necessary wild-goose chase of culture—of which psychoanalysis is a part—can be both depleting and radically dismaying for the individual; and yet the individual has nowhere else to go. He can only know his most private or recondite preoccupations in the public language of culture. His privacy, at best, is a public life in secret.

In describing infantile sexuality in these remarkable early papers, Freud is describing that which it is impossible for us not to be interested in: what it might be—what it was once like—for our curiosity to be irresistible, the kind of artistic vocation that Picasso was referring to when he said, "I don't seek, I find."

IV

Children, using James's earlier terms, live intensely; and their art—the making of sexual theories—"makes life, makes interest, makes importance." In Freud's view, their sexuality, in one sense, *is* their art. Their lives are not sacrificed to theory-making, but rather their lives are made possible by it. Their "importance," which their parents' sexuality threatens, is literally sustained by their family romances. Indeed, one could say that with the concept of sublimation—at least as applied to children and their sexual researches—Freud dissolved the distinction between art and life. Instead of, in Yeats's famous words, the supposed choice between perfection of the life or perfection of the work, there is, Freud suggests, only one thing we cannot help but do, and for which children are our exemplary models, and that is sublimate. Children are exemplary, for Freud in these early papers, because they make of their sexuality an interest in sexuality. So the question posed by James's defense of his art to Wells, and Freud's account of children's sexual researches, is not, to sublimate or not to sublimate? but, what is a good sublimation? What makes a sublimation work—like psychoanalysis itself, say—work sufficiently well for us? What are our individual criteria for this, and where do they come from? Why read Henry James rather than watch pornography— both, of course, sublimations? This is clearly a moral question about the roots and the consequences of our most impassioned interests. And interests, as Freud shows, are never innocent but always morally ambiguous. What Freudian descriptions of a life formulate in a specific way are the senses in which we have official and unofficial interests, and that we are often unaware of the difference (when I'm reading Henry James, I may be reading pornography). As a crude Freudian—a not uninteresting thing to try to be these days—one could say that patients are suffering from not having made good enough sublimations. That they have got further and further away from those things that—for whatever reason— matter most to them. That their official interests— what Freud called "civilized morality"—the "ideals of education"—are spellbinding, their unofficial interests hidden. Their official education has extinguished their unofficial education. It is not always enlivening to be well informed.

If, for example, we think of psychoanalytic (or

any other) training as like Freud's children engaged in their sexual researches, then we are immediately confronted with a puzzle. Each of us, by virtue of the idiosyncrasy of our histories, our present life predicaments, what Freud might call our libidinal stages, have particular, specific, private preoccupations. And yet we are encouraged to—indeed it is a training requirement that we should—read quite a broad range of theory. On any given day, can this page of Lacan, that paper by Sullivan, this concept of Klein's, be meaningful to me? The more diligent self I need for my official education may read it all week by week. From the point of view of my unofficial education—my affinities rather than my duties—it can only be intermittently and unpredictably interesting. We are continually being told the facts of life—the canon of essential psychoanalytic or literary texts, the books professionals need in order to be professional—and yet only some of the facts seem at all nourishing; we can copy them—remember them and reproduce them—but we can't make anything sufficiently our own with them. They are, in other words, minor traumas; not subject to inner transformation. It is the antitransformational objects that are the most dispiriting. Those objects we have no interest in transforming—and so are of no interest—or those objects that demand that we do not transform them but merely abide by them. Absolute obedience is a fear of interest. A trauma, one could say, is a set of bewildering, unconscious instructions.

A good interpretation, by contrast, is something we cannot help remaking (in psychoanalysis the orders the patient is being given are turned into questions). In this sense psychoanalysis, as Laplanche suggests, "de-translates" the patient's material; it undoes the patient's habitual, defensive associations in the service of spontaneous recombinations. Loose ends become newer beginnings.

And yet anyone with a psychoanalytic ear reading all this about the vocation of art—about the Freudian child as our originary artist, about the wonders of passionate curiosity—might begin to feel a certain kind of weary déjà vu; as though we are reentering the twilight home of the sixties, the nostalgic graveyard of certain versions of the Freudian left. And if we want to be fashionable contemporaries, how can we talk about the child—or indeed the adult—having *real* interests when Freud's sense of the human subject is as a site of competing projects? What Richard Rorty calls "a plurality of sets of beliefs and desires," none of them intrinsically more valuable or real than any other except by our making them so. The whole notion of sublimation makes sense only if there is something to sublimate. And yet our description of whatever this is—sexuality, aggression, perversion—is itself a sublimation, a cultural, sharable construction. If we are essentialists of one sort or another, we can say that our childhood selves are our essence, and as children we were essentially interested in sex, or, to put it more scientifically, in our biological destiny. Indeed, one version of what Freud is saying is that we are born essentialists struggling to be more plural, or, as we say, pluralist. In this sense the essentialist—the so-called pervert, or hysteric, or obsessional or narcissist—is immature, has kept himself narrow-minded. Optimally, our development entails reshaping our sexuality into more satisfying forms, finding ways of making excitement and safety sufficiently compatible; what we call pathology is always a narrowing of the psychic field, the stereotyping of erotic imagination.

What I am calling interest is a word for what in psychoanalytic language might be called good-enough sublimation. Sublimation in which the body is only forgotten in order to be better remembered, as in any unselfconscious performance. When we free-associate, we forget ourselves in order to speak. As we understand ourselves more through analysis, we know ourselves less. We forget who we thought we were, or who we thought we needed to be. As one becomes more attentive to the contingencies and determinations of one's life, one's future selves become definite only in their unpredictability. The future will be like the past, not in the sense of repetition, but in the sense of having been uncalculated. So one of the aims of analysis is to free people to do nothing to the future but be interested in it. It is the difference, perhaps, between two kinds of interest, the foreclosed and the genuinely prospective (in psychoanalytic terms, the difference between what the Lacanian child at the mirror stage makes of what he sees in the mirror and what the Winnicottian child might make of the analyst's squiggle).[3] The difference between a conviction and a possible surprise. The now familiar difference between the essentialist and the pluralist. Only our surprises—and those less inviting surprises called traumas—can sabotage our foregone conclusions.

So what I want to make out of Freud's early papers about the child as theorist—the child who is an artist because he wants to be a failed scientist—is a simple proposal: that we should all be essentialists trying to be pluralists, and pluralists trying to be essentialists. That we should want to commit ourselves, as persuasively and eloquently as possible, to both sides of the line at once. That we should sustain the conflict inside us and not be trying to resolve it. From a psychoanalytic point of view, children are essentialists; contemporary adults don't have to be. There is no way of having it without having it both ways. If we don't, we may, like Freud's civilized children, simply lose interest, lose heart, become too eagerly too old for pleasure.

part two

THE BEAST IN THE NURSERY

What moves me is the irregular form—the flawed words and stubborn sounds . . . that affect us whenever we try and say something that is important to us.

—JOHN ASHBERY, *Interview*

I

Psychoanalysis is quintessentially modern in its idealization of "natural" origins—the unconscious, instinct, childhood—and its preoccupation with loss. If desires for satisfaction—an urgent love of life, a commitment to appetite—are assumed to be, one way or another, driving the child into the future, growing up is nevertheless construed as the attenuation of pleasures. Through the displacement and substitution of her desires, the child is all the time giving things up—omnipotence, desire for and dominion over the parents, babbling—in order to secure the supposedly more viable satisfactions of maturity, all of which entail increasingly sophisticated forms of representation. Psychoanalysis has been quintessentially reactionary in its acceptance and promotion of this dismayingly comforting progress myth. We are born in turbulent love with the world, which is assumed to be made for us, of a piece with our wishes; then we suffer the humiliation of disillusionment, in which our rage is the last vestige of our hope. And then, if we are lucky—if we have the character, or the right parents, or both—we accommodate to the insufficiencies. We become the heroes and heroines of our own limitations: masters of absence. And if we are exceptional, we become wise, serene in our enlightened adaptation to the way the world is. Psychoanalysis, in other words, confirms the traditional view that in fact we have been born into the wrong world. But for some reason—salvation, moral well-being, pleasure, genetic transmission—we must try and make the most of it.

This class-blind, politically pacifying, and apparently ahistorical myth of human development—sometimes referred to as the "life cycle," as though it will go on forever—has given some versions of psychoanalysis at least limited credibility in a world increasingly hostile to its values and claims of legitimacy. (So part of the usefulness of psychoanalysis is as a symptomatic profession expressing the muddles of its culture.) Like the child who no longer dares to go "grotesquely astray"—who is no longer capable of a bizarre thought, and is addicted to consensus—this trimming of psychoanalysis has obscured something of value: an attentiveness to the irregular, to the oddity, the unpredictability of what each person makes of what he is given—the singularity born of each person's distinctive history. The sense in which a passionate life is a good life because of its goodness is always in question. In Freud's early work, pre 1912, psychoanalysis was a new way of describing—of sustaining without idealizing—whatever confounded our ways of making sense, whatever held us up (life starting up again where fluency breaks down). In dreams, in slips of the tongue, in children's sexual theories, in symptoms, Freud noticed that people's (moral) coherence, their intelligibility to themselves, was being interfered with, and it was being disrupted by something else in themselves that Freud called "sexuality" or "the unconscious." The ways in which people behaved—the things they actually did—suggested to him that they were in some formative disagreement with themselves; in every symptom or mistake it was as though some internal consensus kept breaking down. We are always doing more and less than we want. Beginning in childhood, we transform our experience according to our conscious projects, and in spite of them. When we talk, what interrupts our theme is as interesting as the theme itself. Psychoanalysis, that is to say, offers us a point of view from which the minor irritation of our momentarily losing the thread, or unnecessarily punning, adds interest (there is something furtive about accuracy). Our mistakes can incite curiosity rather than merely invite punishment: our efficiency can be a refuge.

But in order to make a mistake, of course, one has to know the rules. Error is a function of competence. Or to put it another way, in what sense do young children make mistakes? Because, in a sense, becoming acculturated is learning what it is to make a mistake. Children around nursery age—between two and three years old—are both just learning to speak and just making the momentous transition from family to the first version of school. And one thing this entails, among many others, is a paradoxical form of renunciation for the child. At the time when her curiosity is becoming increasingly sophisticated, it is as though she has to give up what she can never in fact relinquish, her inarticulate self, the self before language (what Seamus Heaney refers to as "pre-reflective lived experience"). As the child embarks upon her own elaborate theory-making—her sexual researches into how to live and who to be— she has in the background, as a kind of taproot, her passionate life without words. At this point in her life the child leaves more than one home, something she will do every time she speaks, which is always out of her own previous silence. That noisy silence, before language joined in, is a lengthy part of her own history. Words are not merely a substitute for wordlessness; they are something else entirely.

Learning to talk is difficult, and it doesn't get any easier. The child at nursery school is at that age when he or she is making for the first, but not the last time, that fateful transition—that can never be complete, that can never be whole-hearted because the renunciation, the loss of the unspoken self is too great—to joining the language group, to participating in the community of apparently competent speakers. "Why are words the thing?" the child might wonder, if it could. "What is learning to speak learning to do, or like learning to do?" Or, to ask a more obviously psychoanalytic question, what exactly must be given up in order to speak? Anyone who works or lives with nursery-age children is confronted by or, rather, reminded of these questions.

But if the adults inevitably teach the children to talk, the children teach (or remind) the adults what it is not to be able to speak. Adults learn from these children what they learn, say, from literature: the struggle, the strain, the apparent concessions, and the erotic delights of articulation, of making one's voices known. The enigma of how words come out of bodies, which is like and unlike whatever else comes in and out of bodies (where words come from, after all, is every bit as perplexing as where babies come from; words can nourish, soothe, excite, and poison their speakers). And how it is not quite clear what the limits of language are limits of. So in a progressivist view of education we would say: the child must learn to speak, to communicate his need. In a nonprogressivist view we would have to add: the child (and the adult) must learn not to speak, must remember what that is like; must be shown how speaking comes out of the unspeaking part of ourselves. The young child will be taught to speak, because he will also notice—or acknowledge through his determined disregard—that there are areas of experience, realms of feeling, that seem resistant to speech, where words might seem inappropriate or ill-suited. Areas in which, as an adult, he may find himself to be either virtually dumb or especially fluent but never exact or original (areas like sex, money, class, or privilege). From a psychoanalytic point of view, the glibness or the silence speak of baffled intensities; resistance is the sign of passion, of curiosities being tempered. If to speak is to speak of what one wants, of what matters most, then to speak is always to run the risk of humiliation. It is a post-

Romantic cliché—which nonsense poetry and surrealism could parody—that adults often lose the inventiveness, the verbal aliveness and mischief, of children. But what children are always encouraged to lose is the knowledge that they do not know how to speak (properly). If you know too well how to do something, you're less likely to fall into originality. Innovation depends upon competence; but competence depends on ignorance. There is nowhere else it can come from.

II

"The majority of children who enter our nursery school," Anna Freud writes, "do so with either absent or inadequate verbalisation of their needs and wishes; instead they express their feelings by means of gestures, actions, temper tantrums and other affective outbursts." This "absent or inadequate verbalisation" she refers to is, in her view, largely the consequence of environmental deprivation—the child's natural capacity to gradually speak his needs undermined by an absence of sufficient nurture. And yet this is also, of course, a description of all our beginnings. "Instead"—an important word here—instead of adequate verbalization, she asserts, the child communicates by way of "gestures, actions, temper tantrums and other affective outbursts."

There are at least two obvious assumptions here; one is that there is such a thing as "adequate verbalization" which brings with it the (aesthetic) question of who decides, and by what criteria, what constitutes adequate, appropriate, good-enough speaking. (We may all be able to recognize it when we hear it, but we may not know quite how we got to have this knack, this trick of consensual good taste.) The whole notion of learning to talk implies that you might know when you can do it. That someone is in a position—call the person, for the sake of it, an adult—to convey to the child that he has competently or successfully expressed himself. The adult who responds to the child's needs—one thing children can't do is bring up children—is inevitably the arbiter of the child's communicative competence. But for the adult to be able to do this, he or she must already know, more or less, what there is in the child to be expressed (we learn from the culture what is assumed to be inside children; psychoanalysts, for example, might say instincts, while neurobiologists would say genes). Because all this is potentially so bewildering—rather like overhearing the free associations in ordinary speech—the adult with a nursery-aged child may not be in a hurry to ask himself, Why do I think, what's made me think at this moment, that this child has expressed himself properly? How have I come to recognize and confirm this as an adequate verbalization? To wonder about this is to be reminded of an ineluctable early conflict between the child and the adult who was once a child. Who decides what I have to say, and whether I have said it? As I will suggest in the next chapter, our most vivid but misleading picture of "adequate verbalization" is the order carried out to the apparent satisfaction of the one who has given it. The issue of "absent or inadequate verbalization" never goes away. It cannot be mastered or developmentally achieved, because such adequacy is always in question, always contestable—even if the contest, in childhood, needs to go underground. The life in us can't escape from itself, even in words.

Children learn very quickly how to make the adults feel that their language makes sense, that it works. But imitation is also the parody that dares not speak its name. ("In painting," Francis Bacon remarked in an interview, "we always leave in too much that is habit, we never eliminate enough. . . .") The habit of speaking properly, of using language more or less like everyone else, takes time to acquire. Language is the cure for infancy, but children take to it with varying degrees of eagerness (and the more severe "pathologies," like autism, are always associated with what is called, perhaps euphemistically, language delay). Indeed, Anna Freud's second, broadly psychoanalytic assumption implies that words are the solution to wordlessness. Nothing terrorizes people more in our culture than the refusal of food and the refusal of words (what would have to happen to a person to make them refuse these two pillars of civilization?). Anna Freud assumes, quite understandably, that there is a progress, a successful sophistication, in the child replacing gestures, actions, tantrums, affective outbursts with language. That the child can acquire some of the content of civilization by containing herself in words. The infantile self is always a rough diamond, and language makes us more . . . what? Understood, manageable, satisfied, communicative, interesting, compliant, competent, appealing, lovable, shameable? There is no sense in Anna Freud's account—as untouched by modern linguistics as Freud's theories—of language as a mixed blessing, no sense that in its own way it protracts, in a radically revised form, all the bafflements and turbulence of gestures and tantrums (be-

cause adults can speak so well they are often unable
to have tantrums; the rant is not an art form). For
Anna Freud language is of the essence (there is no
person worth speaking of before it); there is an un-
equivocal advantage to be gained for the child from
what she calls, in a section entitled "The Nursery
School's Role in Promoting Verbalization," "a maximum of carefully planned verbal interactions with
the child." In a title about verbalization the word
"promoting" seems of interest with its meaning both
of furthering the progress of, but also of advertising,
of putting on a show. By speaking, one might say, the
child advertises his civility; he puts off the old Adam
and puts on a show of humane adequacy.

I'm exaggerating this because I want to draw attention to what is concealed by myths of progress, or
so-called developmental achievement, and to show
how psychoanalysis has itself been compromised by
its commitment to adaptation as opposed to (not instead of) innovation. Psychoanalysis—as both theory
and practice—can also dispirit people by making
them better able to endure their ungainly fit with the
culture (being able to bear the people and the institutions we depend upon is called masochism). The
reassuring fictions of so-called insight—the how-I-
came-to-be-who-I-am stories—are a poor substitute

for people's capacity to transform their worlds (as children do in their theory-making, and as we all do in dreamwork). Psychoanalysis should not be promoting knowledge as a consolation prize for injustice.

It is clear that the child obviously gained a great deal from Anna Freud's "maximum of carefully planned verbal interactions with the child," which ranged, as she says, "from the simple naming of objects in the room or in the picture book to sophisticated storytelling and to communication in the so-called 'talking circle' where each child learned to report to fellow pupils on happenings at home, on personal opinions and experiences." We don't need to idealize the child as some noble savage or primitive poet ruined by the talking circle of culture; after all, where else could he learn the pleasure of talking, and who else could he talk to? Indeed, culture makes our objections to culture possible. But what psychoanalysis, as part of this culture, can show us—as, perhaps, can Darwinism, in a different way—is the conflict and collaboration inside each person between an absence of verbalization (not precultural so much as protocultural) and a relative fluency, between a part of the self that can and sometimes wants to speak, and a part of the self that is verbally confounded (not merely adversarial to the culture but at odds with it). Learning to talk entails keeping alive the inarticulate self, a self capable of astonishing states of satisfaction and amazing rage at their absence. "No one who has seen a baby sinking back satiated from the breast," Freud writes in an infamous passage in *Three Essays on the Theory of Sexuality,* "and falling asleep with flushed cheeks and a blissful smile can escape the reflection that this picture persists as a prototype of the expression of sexual satisfaction in later life." If this is a prototype, then no one can also escape from the reflection that it is a preverbal one. For the satisfied, speaking adult the precursor and model for her satisfaction was perhaps a wordless state, but made known in language.

III

Learning to speak is not the same as learning another language. It would be misleading to assume that young children are involved in an act of translation; words are not merely translations of sounds, so what is translated? It is not simply one life in terms of another, because that other passionate life had no terms. It was articulated without words. As the young child becomes gradually more verbally coherent—less impressed by her uncivil self—she is forever crossing and recrossing the borders of articulation; both learning the language games and noticing the odd fit between language and what happens. Anyone who spends time with nursery-age children knows the sheer scale of their emotional impact, how they both experience and arouse— often with daunting speed and fluency—the most passionate and therefore puzzling feelings. In small children, it is as though love and hate, among many other things, are in continual exchange with each other. So it is not entirely surprising that the adults can be in a bit of a hurry to get beyond the child's wordlessness, which is so reminiscent of their own, nor, indeed, that they overidentify with, and so overencourage the child's more verbally competent future selves. For the young child the future is language. But as psychoanalysts, among others, know, the future is not exactly the solution for the past. We need only think of the tricky part that words play in our erotic encounters if we want to redescribe the predicament of the young child and the adults who look after him. There is the uneasy marriage of word and desire, and there are the ways in which words fail us that can only be described in words.

And there is the emotional turbulence—the sheer impact people can have on each other—that words can seem unsuitable for, or for which language is only useful in retrospect. The child whom we delight in as a new speaker is also the child we fear might refuse to play the game, or who simply might not have the words. The adult analogies—not finding the word for something, being struck dumb or buried alive—are all stories of loss, not of this formative absence the child at first thrives in. For the infant and young child—from their point of view, as it were—language is not missing (what is to be mourned is the prelinguistic self). But what the adults call intense feeling is present, and unavoidable.

Young children are apprentice, often dilettante, speakers. Amateurs of the sentence, they cannot help but unwittingly experiment with language, because they can only learn the rules—the conventions of syntax and diction—by, from the adult's point of view, breaking them. But at the same time, they teach us what it is like not to be able to speak properly; and by showing us this they remind us not only of our inarticulate and virtually inarticulate selves, but also of our internal relationship with these buried, vestigial versions of ourselves. Anyone who

lives or works with small children knows how evocative linguistic incompetence is; how inventive, how
surprising, how exasperating, how frustrating it is.
Indeed, our relationship to children of this formative
age—how we manage and respond to the ways in
which they unsurely speak to us and each other—is
one picture of our relationship to our own pre- and
virtually linguistic selves. These children take us back
to that border in ourselves where we struggle or delight to articulate against powerful external and internal resistances. And the complementary risk is
that adults use young children unwittingly, to rein-
force a sense of their own competence (like the
analyst who interprets in order to feel securely
knowledgeable).

"Words," the psychoanalyst J. B. Pontalis writes in
his autobiography, *Love of Beginnings,* "do not come
from words." With young children, as they speak and
refuse to speak, as they experiment with words and
give up on them, we witness with extraordinary im-
mediacy words coming from somewhere. We might
call it the body, or we might refer to it as an indeterminate place where the bodily self meets that con-
tagion of languages called culture. Every time we
speak, and perhaps particularly every time we have

difficulty speaking—and so get a glimpse of what our fluency conceals—we are connected unconsciously with that period when we started speaking. Clearly, one of the reasons stammers and other speech impediments are so powerfully poignant or unsettling is that they confront us too starkly with our passion for hesitation, with that formative difficulty of getting the words out, under pressure. They link us with a verbally less resourceful but emotionally abundant time of our lives, when we were full of pauses and hesitations, when we could be apoplectic with rage and were capable of bliss, "cradled by tempests," in Shelley's phrase.

Clearly, in this crossover to language from whatever we imagine precedes it—and our stories about the preverbal child are as cultured, as made up out of what's there, as accounts of any of our developmental stages—the child can both elaborate her curiosity and begin to experience the learned behavior of shame, guilt, and humiliation. The child's urgent wanting—that is, her love of the future—is attenuated. Acknowledging the existence of other people—which in psychoanalysis is redescribed as acknowledging one's dependence on other people—entails a tempering of the self.

What are variously described in the psychoanalytic literature as disillusionment, narcissistic rage, the depressive position, are all versions of a familiar story—that the viable self is a diminished self. (In a curious cultural inversion, modern babies are described, and so often experienced, as both imperialists and commodities by their parents.) Growing up then becomes the necessary flight from inarticulateness, from the less affectively organized self, a self without its best behaviors to be on, a self that suffers and enjoys at a pitch that the grown-ups often find daunting. In the old, modern fable of civilization and its discontents, either the child or the culture is demonized. But if we redescribe development as not simply the progressive acquisition of linguistic, and therefore moral, competence, we may be better able to nurture in children the necessary to-and-fro between the inarticulate and the articulate selves; a to-and-fro that might be sustainable throughout life rather than having its last gasp during adolescence, or in mystical states, which are always subject to so much fascination and suspicion by those who ironize them (so-called perversion is always a compromised mysticism).

There is, Wordsworth writes in his note to "The Thorn," "a consciousness of the inadequateness of our own powers, or the deficiencies of language" in any attempt to "communicate impassioned feelings." This is exactly what we witness and what is re-evoked in us by children beginning to speak. In a political ethos increasingly committed to communication technology—to efficient development (as productivity), both psychological and economic—psychoanalysis is one way of speaking up for our formative linguistic incompetence, for the necessary relationship between our verbal uncertainty and our fluency, for the profit of loss. It is a paradox perhaps best captured in music (or tones of voice) that it is sounds and silence that link us to our earliest states of being. Our parents may have spoken words to us as babies, but they were not words to us.

It is of course possible to facilitate in the child a tolerance of, and a pleasure in, verbal insufficiency (getting it wrong is only humiliating if there is some-one powerful who has an intransigent need for it to be right). The concise formulation, the incisive ex-planation—just like a lucid interpretation in analy-sis—can be a misleading picture for the child and indeed a strain, an impossible demand on the child's emerging powers of representation (as Blake wrote, "What is not too explicit is the fittest for instruction because it rouses the faculties to act"). The nursery-age child is not struggling for clarity; he is struggling for articulation. The child's most pressing messages are likely to be obscure and ambiguous. So, for example, doing psychoanalysis with children of this age involves acknowledging a paradox: that one is facilitating communications that are the most difficult to understand (or whose reception cannot be captured by the word "understanding"); that the young child, like the adult who claims to interpret her, is only ever verging on sense. In the young child's speech—as in the free association of adults—one hears things at once nonconsensual but not nonsense. This is what the critic Lucy Newlyn means when she refers to "the importance of linguistic inadequacy . . . for imaginative success." "Emotional or intellectual intensity," she writes, ". . . correlates with verbal insufficiency." Rewarding certain kinds of fluency, the relatively clear communication of needs and wants, shores up our confidence in the talking circle, and, indeed, our wishful and unfounded belief in the potential clarity of wanting. And it can make the child unduly troubled by not being able to speak, and unduly terrorized by the prearticulate selves that, as it were, insist on their importance—and their embodiment—in sexuality and illness. The commonsense question "Who am I?"

may be answerable in words. The psychoanalytic question "If I'm not exactly what I think I am, then what else can I be?" unavoidably complicates our relationship to language.

IV

Asked by a *Paris Review* interviewer whether he wrote in longhand, Ted Hughes answered the question by way of a piece of autobiography, talking both about his own childhood and his experience of other children's writing. "I made an interesting discovery about myself," Hughes said,

when I first worked for a film company. I had to write brief summaries of novels and plays to give the directors some idea of their film potential—a page or so of prose about each book or play, and then my comment. That was where I began to write for the first time directly onto a type-writer. I was then about twenty-five. I realised instantly that when I composed directly onto the type-writer my sentences became three times as long, much longer. My subordinate clauses flowered

Adam Phillips

and multiplied and ramified away down the length of the page, all much more eloquently than anything I would have written by hand. Recently I made another similar discovery. For about thirty years I've been on the judging panel of the W. H. Smith children's writing competition. . . . Usually the entries are a page, two pages, three pages. That's been the norm. Just a poem or a bit of prose, a little longer. But in the early 1980's we suddenly began to get seventy and eighty page works. These were usually space fiction, always very inventive and always extraordinarily fluent—a definite impression of a command of words and prose, but without exception strangely boring. It was almost impossible to read them through. After two or three years, as these became more numerous, we realised that this was a new thing. So we enquired. It turned out that these were pieces that children had composed on word processor. What's happening is that as the actual tools for getting words onto the page become more flexible and externalised, the writer can get down almost every thought, or every extension of thought. That ought to be an advantage. But in fact, in all these cases, it just extends everything slightly too much. Every sentence is too long. Everything is taken a bit too far, too attenuated. There's always a bit too much there and it's too thin. Whereas when writing by hand you meet the terrible resistance of what happened your first year at it when you couldn't write at all . . . when you were making attempts, pretending to form letters. These ancient feelings are there, wanting to be expressed. When you sit with your pen, every year of your life is right there, wired into the communication between your brain and your writing hand. There is a natural characteristic resistance that produces a certain kind of result analogous to your actual handwriting. As you force your expression against the built-in resistance, things become automatically more compressed, more summary and, perhaps, psychologically denser.

Clearly, a lot could be said here about the links between the children's "command of words," with all it implies of a spurious kind of sovereignty, and their strangely boring writing; about how some forms of modern technology reshape the imagination. And more pertinent to the theme of this book, how sitting with a pen in your hand would mean, at least until recently, "every year of your life is right there, wired into the communication between your brain and your writing hand." But there are of course no comparable technological aids to speaking. I may graduate from a pencil to a pen to a typewriter to a word processor as my writing evolves, but I am only ever going to speak with my mouth. As psychoanalysis would suggest, the prehistory of my mouth, in relation to the necessary other people that make up my first world, is every bit as important for my speech as the technological development of my writing. And in this sense one could say that the arts connect us more starkly to earlier stages of development; we fingerpaint before we can use a microscope, we babble before we can do math.

Breathing, eating, babbling, singing, and speaking make a puzzling continuum of experience; we are always at, or on, the oral stage wherever else we are. What kind of meals does the child make of words? They come out of his mouth, but in what sense do they go into his mouth, like food and air? Are words something spat out? How does the child digest both the language he is being offered and the language going on around him? From a psychoanalytic point of view these are questions about any particular child's largely unconscious fantasy about the work-ings of bodies in relationship. If we prioritize, on the child's behalf, as it were, body-based analogies, we will be wondering what speaking and listening are like for the child (being penetrated, being soothed, being taken in, spoiling, and so on). And we may also be able to differentiate between offering children words they can do, or make, something of their own with (words as hints) and words they can only sub-mit to or reject (words as orders). There is a differ-ence between words you can digest and words you can only copy, a difference between poetry and slo-gans. To be parents or teachers (or psychoanalysts) rather than merely autocrats or bullies, we need to distinguish between vocabularies that are to be imi-tated—that offer themselves up as fetishes, or for identification (being like the kind of person who speaks like this)—and vocabularies that invite trans-formation (the difference, say, between a poem and an instruction manual). And we need to consider the preconditions—the kinds of relationship—that sponsor or obstruct individual innovation. One of Freud's models for that was, as I have said, the dreamwork, with its strange product of the dream. Made out of culturally recognizable material, the dream manages both to be evocative and to confound our ordinary sense of the intelligible. If we nurture the inarticulate self in the nursery-age child, she will become less intelligible but more communicative, an evoker rather than, or as well as, an informer, in the to-and-fro between using language and being unable to, between making sense and losing the thread. Dreamwork, in other words—and in a different but complementary way, Winnicott's notion of object-usage—may be better models for learning a language that feels worth speaking, that, in Winnicott's telling phrase, "feels real." [4]

The Freudian child is informed by preverbal experience, and dreams the uneasy fit between passion and reality. He dreams visually, sees his dreams without looking, and can only report them in words (if they were painted, with no verbal commentary, we wouldn't know it was a dream). In dreaming, in making up sexual theories, and in what Winnicott calls object-usage, it is as though the child says: "I don't know what's true, I only know what it interests me to believe, what satisfies my curiosity. I know how to speak but I only want to say what's real to me." The Freudian child, in other words, a pragmatist and a dreamer, can only be taught what he wants to know.

V

For Freud psychoanalysis was essentially about the fate of interest, about how each person sustains, or fails to sustain—attacks, sabotages, or gives up on—their appetite for life (to be interested in appetite is to be interested in people's relationship to hope). In some contemporary versions of psychoanalysis this turns into the question, what has to happen to people to make them feel that the world is a promising place to live in? Or, what do we need now to acknowledge about ourselves in order to make our lives seem viable, or even plausible? Whether contemporary psychoanalysts describe themselves as problem solvers or pursuers of truth, they are always dealing with how certain things have come to matter to people, and whether these hierarchies of value work well enough in the stories people are telling themselves about their lives, about how they make good their lives.

In a talk given in 1950 to psychology and social-work students entitled "Yes, but How Do We Know It's True?" the British psychoanalyst D. W. Winnicott suggested that there were two stages people always

go through when they are taught psychology. "In the
first stage," he writes,

> they learn what is being taught about psy-
> chology just as they learn other things. In the
> second stage the psychological teaching begins
> to separate out from the other as something
> that just can't be learnt. It has to be felt as real,
> or else it is irritating, or even maddening.

The first stage of learning can be called, in
Freud's language, identification; the student becomes
like somebody who knows these things. In Winnicott's language it would be called compliance; the
child fits in with the teacher's need to teach, and, by
implication, with the culture's demand that these
are the things one learns, and this is the way one
learns them. In the first stage, that is to say, the
student adapts to what is supposedly the subject
being taught. At this stage competence is a kind of
imitation; the context defines the project.

In the second stage something akin to what Freud
calls dreamwork, and Winnicott differently calls
object-usage, goes on. Each student, consciously and
unconsciously, makes something of his own out of it
all; finds the bits he can use, the bits that make per-

sonal sense. The teaching experience is radically re-contextualized according to personal need. He has to find, and make, the parts of the subject (if any) that are of value to him. As in Winnicott's description of object-usage, the student attacks the subject with questions and criticisms, and finds out what's left after the assault; whatever survives this critique—this hatred—is felt to be of real substance (resilient, incorruptible, worth banking on). In this way the student makes (or fails to make) psychology true for him. In the terms of Freud's account of dreamwork the subject matter, the teaching, is like what Freud calls the dream day, in which, quite unbeknownst to ourselves, we are selecting material for the night's dream. As if, while we go about our official business, an artist inside us is all the time on the lookout for material to make a dream with. So from the point of view of the dreamwork, the student finds himself unwittingly drawn to specific bits of the subject being taught—whatever the emphasis of the teacher happens to be—which he will then, more or less secretly (even to himself), transform into something rather strange. If he did this while he was asleep, we would call it a dream; if he does it while he is awake, it will be called a misunderstanding, a delusion, or an original contribution to the subject.

In other words, in the second stage the student makes the subject fit in with his or her unconscious project. He uses it for self-fashioning, or he dispenses with it. The first stage that Winnicott describes might be called the student's official education; the second stage, whether one redescribes it as object-usage or dreamwork, may be rather more like the student's unofficial education.

In one sense Winnicott's notion of object-usage is entirely compatible with the principles, if not the practice, of liberal education; liberal institutions favoring, as they claim to do, debate and critique and the democratic (or agonistic) formulation of criteria of value. Freud's dreamwork, however—to which Winnicott's useful concept is affiliated—has more radical implications for our stories about learning and teaching. One implication is that people can learn but they can't be taught, or, at least, they can't be taught anything of real significance. And that is partly because no one can ever know beforehand— neither themselves nor their teachers—exactly what is of personal significance; that is, exactly what a person will find significant, select out to dream with, to remember or to forget; to work on. What is of interest to someone—what Freud called their "preconditions for loving"—is both recondite and profoundly idiosyncratic, a function of the strange weaving of personal history and unconscious desire. Unpredictable, and intelligible, if at all, only in retrospect. Because self-knowledge is always a reconstruction, it is always out of date. The self is a thing of the past.

From a psychoanalytic point of view, I have my conscious preoccupations and ambitions, and these make me more or less educable. But I also have my unconscious desires and affinities—tropisms and drifts of attention—that can be quite at odds with my conscious ideals. I may go to a lecture on psychology and be fascinated; but I may dream that night about the earrings of the woman sitting next to me, which, if I were to associate to this detail in the dream might, like Proust's legendary madeleine, open up vistas of previously unacknowledged personal history. So in Freud's view, virtue can be taught, but only to a part of the self (in Freud's metapsychology the superego is internalized initially from the parents, and then the ego has morality, as it were, forced upon it by the superego and through its own adaptation to its circumstances). Other, more or equally powerful parts of the self—called variously by Freud the id (basic instinct) or, more inclusively, the unconscious (id plus dreaming self)—are either recalcitrant to influence or are living by their own rules (though quite where they learn these rules Freud never considers; they could only come from the culture). The ego and to a far lesser extent the superego in this Freudian story are both, by definition, educable and keen to learn. Indeed, from the ego's point of view, acculturation is tantamount to survival (contemporary child psychotherapists always want to know whether the child is learning well in school). But it is what I am calling the dreaming self—with its dreamwork and its idiosyncratic desire—that is the new Freudian contribution to the traditional questions about education (virtue, for example, cannot be taught; it can only be suggested). From the point of view of the dreaming self, learning is a sublimation of desiring; there is no learning without desire, or none, in Winnicott's language, that is "felt as real." The dreaming self cannot be schooled in the traditional sense because it always chooses its teachers; any available cultural canon is simply like the dream day for the dreamer (in this sense, the dreamer is always deschooling society). From an unknowable (unconscious) set of criteria a person, unbeknown even to himself, picks out and transforms the bits he wants; the bits that can be used in the hidden projects of unconscious desire

(we are bound to our lives by the feeling we have for
ourselves). In this process, that is like a kind of sleep-
walking solitary self-education, the Freudian subject
is, as it were, the Victorian autodidact romanticized.
Dreamwork is unforced labor.

So when Freud came to write about children's education, he wrote more, and more interestingly,
about children's self-education, about what they
learned despite the adults, not because of them.
Indeed, Freud's implicit paradigm for teaching and
learning—in which he was also alluding to the prob-
lematic teaching and learning of psychoanalysis itself—was the way children conducted what he called
their "sexual researches." The ways in which children acquired their sexual theories, and the forms
these theories took, were the daylight equivalent of
nighttimes of dreamwork. Children, Freud realized,
couldn't really be taught about sex—they could only
teach themselves, find out in their own ways, according to their own needs at the time. And because in
Freud's view sex, in its fullest sense, was all the child
wanted to know about, learning about sex was the
paradigm for learning (it is part of desiring to be
curious about desire; and to be curious about desire
is to be curious about the future, about what one
is looking forward to). But if children learn about

sex in the same way that they dream, how can they be taught? (Imagine trying to teach someone how to dream.) In other words, for the child as for the adult, the facts of life are a hint as well as an order. Children dream, but adults want to, indeed need to, teach them: children know what interests them, but adults want them educated.

By dramatizing in this way a war between childhood curiosity and education, Freud was describing his version of Romanticism, of what he would later call, in his great elegy for happiness and self-knowledge, "civilization and its discontents." But by doing it in this way—by taking seriously the child's unofficial education of sexual research—Freud confronts us with an interesting set of questions: What would education look like if we took dreaming and children's sexual curiosity as the model for teaching and learning? What would our interest in things and people be like if we thought of our adult selves as more like dreamers and children, as Freud describes them? If we thought of ourselves, in other words, as people who were only prepared to take a hint?

part three

A STAB AT HINTING

If children could follow the hints given by the
excitation of the penis they would get a little
nearer to the solution of the problem.

—FREUD, *On the Sexual Theories of Children*

I

It would be merely cute to be merely suggestive about hinting. And suggestion, as we know, has always been a dirty word in psychoanalysis; even if it has inevitably been the unconscious or its derivatives that were, indeed could only be, suggestive, in need of interpretation. A suggestion, just like a hint, will misfire if no one is tempted to take it up.

So I want to try to do something more definitive; I want to have a stab at hinting, in the knowledge that there could be nothing more absurd than to have the last word on hinting. As though one might want to put a stop to it. A hint, like a dream, tantalizes us with the problem of interpretation, of what it would be to get it right, and where the criteria come from.

Because a theory of hinting—which is one thing psychoanalysis is—will perhaps inevitably tend toward closure, I want to begin with three prepsychoanalytic tableaux, three untheoretical stories about hinting, stories which wouldn't quite work without this key word being somehow the heart of the matter.

To his friend Reynolds, Keats writes on February 19, 1818:

My dear Reynolds,

I have an idea that a Man might pass a very pleasant life in this manner—let him on any certain day read a certain Page of full Poesy or distilled Prose and let him wander with it, and muse upon it, and reflect from it, and bring home to it, and prophesy upon it, and dream upon it—untill it becomes stale—but when will it do so? Never—When Man has arrived at a certain ripeness in intellect any one grand and spiritual passage serves him as a starting post towards all "the two-and thirty Pallaces." How happy is such a "voyage of conception," what delicious diligent Indolence! A doze upon a Sofa does not hinder it, and a nap upon Clover engenders ethereal finger-pointings— the prattle of a child gives it wings, and the converse of middle age a strength to beat them—a strain of musick conducts to "an odd angle of the Isle" and when the leaves whisper it puts a "girdle round the earth." Nor will this sparing touch of noble Books be any irrever- ance to their Writers—for perhaps the honors

paid by Man to Man are trifles in comparison
to the Benefit done by great Works to the
"Spirit and pulse of good" by their mere passive existence. Memory should not be called
knowledge—Many have original Minds who
do not think it—they are led away by
Custom—Now it appears to me that almost
any Man may like the Spider spin from his
own inwards his own airy Citadel—the points
of leaves and twigs on which the Spider begins
her work are few and she fills the Air with a
beautiful circuiting: man should be content
with as few points to tip with the fine Webb of
his Soul and weave a tapestry empyrean—full
of Symbols for his spiritual eye, of softness for
his spiritual touch, of space for his wandering
of distinctness for his Luxury—But the Minds
of Mortals are so different and bent on such
diverse Journeys that it may at first appear impossible for any common taste and fellowship
to exist between two or three under these sup-
positions—It is however quite the contrary—
Minds would leave each other in contrary
directions, traverse each other in Numberless
points, and all [for "at"] last greet each other
at the Journeys end—A old Man and a child

would talk together . . . and Man should not
dispute or assert but whisper results to his
neighbour, and thus by every germ of Spirit
sucking the Sap from mould ethereal every
human might become great, and Humanity
instead of being a wide heath of Furse and
Briars with here and there a remote Oak or
Pine, would become a grand democracy of
Forest Trees. It has been an old Comparison
for our urging on—the Bee hive—however it
seems to me that we should rather be the
flower than the Bee—for it is a false notion
that more is gained by receiving than giving—
no the receiver and the giver are equal in their
benefits—The f[l]ower I doubt not receives a
fair guerdon from the Bee—its leaves blush
deeper in the next spring—and who shall say
between Man and Woman which is the most
delighted? Now it is more noble to sit like Jove
that [for "than"] to fly like Mercury—let us
not therefore go hurrying about and collecting
honey-bee like, buzzing here and there impatiently from a knowledge of what is to be arrived at; but let us open our leaves like a flower
and be passive and receptive—budding patiently under the eye of Apollo and taking

hints from every noble insect that favors us
with a visit—sap will be given us for Meat and
dew for drink—I was led into these thoughts,
my dear Reynolds, by the beauty of the morning operating on a sense of Idleness—I have
not read any Books—the Morning said I was
right—I had no Idea but of the Morning and
the Thrush said I was right.

This is a letter, one could say, about how little one
might need; about what we can learn from insects
about how to live (spiders are exemplary, bees are
not); about indolence and invention and, of course,
about how to read (given a chance, less can be
more).

In this great letter Keats—whose life was tram-
meled by struggle but who was keen to be tena-
cious—is speaking up for, and talking himself into,
the virtue of not being conventionally thorough: he
is writing as a poet, not as a scholar. His letter is a
small manifesto against conscientiousness; in favor
of what psychoanalysts might call dreamwork and
Keats calls, more winningly, diligent indolence.
Because he is for growth, he asserts, he is against
effort (the letter is rife with images of eating,
pollination, and generation). It is a celebration of

affinities—the noble insect that happens to be drawn to the flower—but not of forced relations. What you don't feel like doing, you don't feel like: to be avid with purpose—like the bee "buzzing here and there impatiently from a knowledge of what is to be arrived at"—is a distraction.

Of course, Keats is feeling guilty and needs permission for this hymn to intelligent laziness: "I have not read any Books—the Morning said I was right." There may be guilt about not working, and there may also be guilt about the pleasure of not working. Just as usury was once condemned because it seemed to be a way of earning money without actually working, so the pleasure of dreamwork—a night sleeping, or a day drifting—can seem illicit, a kind of unearned work. We don't always know when we are working or, indeed, what working is. Our ends are often incommensurate with our means.

What Keats is at his most leisured pains to say in this letter is how much can be made of what is apparently so little. You don't have to do very much to get things done as long as you don't need to know what you are doing. If you have too much of a plan, you've got a real job on your hands. Only "a certain Page of full Poesy or distilled Prose" need be mulled over in "delicious diligent Indolence" (it's the difference, say, between reading a book for the sentences and reading it for the plot). "The points of leaves and twigs on which the Spider begins her work are few," and yet from these few points—a not unincidental word—she builds her "own airy Citadel." We need not be busy with intentions, harassed by our aims, but rather, he suggests, "passive and receptive—budding patiently under the eye of Apollo and taking hints from every noble insect that favors us with a visit." This is why it is better to be a flower than a bee; a flower can take a hint. For Keats, inspiration means being able to take the hint.

Keats's letter does what it describes; it even does what Keats wanted it to do for Reynolds: "It is no matter whether I am right or wrong either one way or another, if there is sufficient to lift a little time from your Shoulders." What is sufficient in this letter, for the purposes of this chapter, is two questions Keats leaves us with: What is it to take a hint? And what are the preconditions for being able to do so? Especially, as Keats intimates, when taking a hint, unlike, say, getting a joke, is not a question of right or wrong. That is to say, you cannot be given a hint,

you can only take one, at least in the sense in which
Keats is talking.

———

In his now famous essay "The Art of Fiction,"
published in *Longman's Magazine* in 1884, Henry
James also wrote about what makes for inspiration:

> It is equally excellent and inconclusive to
> say that one must write from experience. To
> our suppositious aspirant [writer] such a decla-
> ration might savour of mockery. What kind of
> experience is intended, and where does it
> begin and end? Experience is never limited
> and it is never complete; it is an immense sen-
> sibility, a kind of huge spider web of the finest
> silken threads suspended in the chamber of
> consciousness, and catching every air-borne
> particle in its tissue. It is the very atmosphere
> of the mind; and when the mind is imagina-
> tive—much more when it happens to be that
> of a man of genius—it takes to itself the
> faintest hints of life, it converts the very pulses
> of the air into revelations. . . . The glimpse
> made a picture; it lasted only a moment, but

that moment was experience . . . [a] direct personal impression.

James refers several times in his prefaces and
notebooks to what he calls the "germ" that set off a
story in him; often it is simply a heard or an over-
heard piece of dinner conversation. He writes, for
example, that *What Maisie Knew* was "another in-
stance of the growth of the great oak from the little
acorn." It was, he writes in his preface, "at least a
tree that spreads beyond any provision its small germ
might on a first handling have appeared likely to
make for it." The germ, the little acorn, was "the accidental mention" of a child and its divorced parents; it was, as his notebooks show, told him at
second hand over dinner. He took the hint, though
of course Mrs. Ashton, who "mentioned to me a situation of which she had known, of which it immediately struck me that something might be made
in a tale," knew nothing of what she had done.
Indeed, how could she have known? If James had sat
next to someone else, he might not have written the
story.

Quite unbeknown to her, James's companion had
prompted something in him; but judging by the
speed of it all, he was ripe for prompting. In the pas-

sage I quoted from "The Art of Fiction," there is
once again, as in Keats's letter, the image of a spider-
web, an image of passive predation, of a readiness. It
waits—by definition it can't know exactly what it is
waiting for—but it knows when it's got something,
something edible, something it is in a hurry to digest
(we might call it dream food). James is describing a
kind of actively alert, passively available act of transformation, not unlike Freud's dreamwork. The story
is instantly something he can use (as with Keats, the
moment of conception is without effort). It "*takes to itself* the faintest hints of life"; "it *converts* the very pulses
of the air into revelations." Like Keats, James is referring to something minimal—not just hints but
faint ones, not lingering looks but glimpses—and the
virtual excess such minima can provoke. It is not only
a tuned responsiveness; it is also an unconscious
radar for affinities, for what speaks to one by calling
up one's own voice (that is how you know that something or someone speaks to you, *it makes you speak*). For
James, it is literally like being called to do something
(just as a good interpretation in analysis makes you,
irresistibly invites you, to associate). But it depends
on the given thing, or what we can sometimes make
of what is given. The paradox James hints at here is

that the useful hint is, more often than not, not intended as such. (Hints, one might say, are freely taken in the sense that they are not felt as compromising.) As far as we know, Mrs. Ashton was not intending to give James a story; she was merely telling him one. As may be coming clear, this has interesting consequences for analysis. Only a god—an all-knowing one—would be able to predict what a person might be able to use. It would be like giving somebody a transitional object for a birthday present, or pointing out a day residue they could use for their night's dream.

If Keats and James are preoccupied by what one might be lucky enough to get and what one has the capacity to use—by the inevitable relationship between imagination and contingency—my final example is about the dangers of overeating, the distraction of too much, of what can happen if you read the whole book instead of dipping into it, the risks of concentrating for too long. In October of 1949, Ludwig Wittgenstein was invited by the philosopher O. K. Bouwsma to talk at Smith College in Massachusetts. They went for a walk together one afternoon, and Wittgenstein started talking about teaching ethics:

Later as we stopped on the hill looking down over the city, he asked me: Had I read any Kierkegaard? I had. He had read some. Kierkegaard is very serious. But he could not read him much. He got hints. He did not want another man's thought all chewed. A word or two was sometimes enough. But Kierkegaard struck him almost of common life. Take his prayers. They left him unmoved. But he once read the prayers and meditations of Samuel Johnson. They were his meat. "The violent incursions of evil thoughts." (I'm not sure about his judgment here of Kierkegaard.) Later, walking in the hills, he returned to the way in which we borrow—hints. He had seen a play, a third-rate, poor play, when he was twenty-two. One detail in that play had made a powerful impression upon him. It was a trifle. But here some peasant, some ne'er-do-well says in the play: "Nothing can hurt me." That remark went through him and now he remembers it. It started things. You can't tell. The most important things just happen to you.

Clearly, there is a lot here that is of interest; like Keats and James, when Wittgenstein starts talking about how to do something—in this case, not how to write but how to teach ethics—he talks about hinting. The hint facilitates something in him, and he places it in opposition to a certain kind of attention that gives him too much contact with the author he is interested in. He could not read Kierkegaard "much." "He did not want another man's thought all chewed. A word or two was sometimes enough." There is an interesting ambiguity in the account: is it that he doesn't want to read too much Kierkegaard, or too much of Kierkegaard chewing on his own thoughts? Whichever it is, too much chewing is bad for the digestion—that is, figuratively, bad for the capacity to think one's own thoughts (what Keats in his letter called being "led away by Custom"). A word or two can make you think; any more and you could feel usurped, force-fed, too full.

It also seems pertinent that Wittgenstein links hinting to borrowing, to taking something of somebody else's for your own use. Certainly, taking it out of their presence (we don't talk about the analysand borrowing the analyst's interpretations, but perhaps we should: nothing is ever returned in the state which it is taken). And along with this goes the more unpremeditated borrowing—referred to by Keats and James—of quite unexpectedly being struck by something, feeling it spoke to you. Perhaps most significant of all is Wittgenstein's point that the value of the hint is irrespective of its apparent aesthetic value. That whatever it is in oneself that is struck by these things has a quite different set of criteria of value. A peasant in a poor play makes a preposterous and bland remark—"Nothing can hurt me"—and yet, it "went through him and now he remembers it. It started things." Hints start things off; and we have no idea beforehand what might be a hint for us. We are doubly helpless; we need hints to get things going, and, as Wittgenstein says, we "can't tell" either what they will be, or what they might start off in us. "The most important things just happen to you," Wittgenstein says; or, as a Freudian might say, we are profoundly unconscious of who we are—of what we might be moved by—and of what we might become, of where our affinities—our psychic affiliations—might come from, and where they may lead us. Like a cue, each hint furthers the drama; but the play is not one we can know.

Keats, James, and Wittgenstein—though all heroes of what might have once been called High Culture—are all talking about something absolutely ordinary, about how the culture they both partly created and contributed to thrived on the everyday. We have all had the experience they describe, of getting the hint. It is presumably obvious by now that hinting links ordinary conversation, and reading, to what goes on in analysis. From a psychoanalytic point of view, these three writers are describing one version of a good interpretation—something the patient can use to make something of his own, something that, by using, the patient discovers what is his to make. And yet it is rather more complicated than this might suggest because, traditionally, we might think that it is the patient who hints—unconsciously through his associations—and the analyst who does something that isn't called hinting, that translates the patient's hints and is called interpretation. And, as all three of these writers insist, the most valuable hints—the ones you can work with, the ones that spark something off in you—may be given unintentionally. The calculated hint would be a contradiction in terms; the good hint is always in the eye of the beholder. And these hints are freely taken, in the sense that they are not felt as compromising, but as a kind of release. How could anyone know, least of all you, what will really work on you? You can acquire a sense of what turns you on—indeed, you might be in too much of a hurry to find out—but you can still be surprised. The fear of pleasure can blind one to its prompts.

A hint, the Oxford English Dictionary suggests, is "an occasion, an opportunity. A slight indication: a suggestion or implication conveyed covertly but intelligibly." It would be possible to discriminate between analytic schools on the basis of the analyst's freedom to hint, or the analyst's relationship to suggestiveness (changing the lengths of sessions, say). But then, as Keats and James and Wittgenstein suggest, only the patient will be able to decide if hinting is what the analyst is doing. After all, not everything may be intended as a hint, but anything might be experienced as one. "The most important things just happen to you." A good interpretation, one might say, is something not intended as a hint by the analyst but taken as one by the patient.

II

A man in his early thirties—a successful merchant banker—referred himself to me because he felt "mildly depressed" when his most recent girlfriend had left him. He was surprised to be feeling like this; he even drifted into thinking about her when he was at work: "No woman," he told me with what was clearly fading bravado, "has ever stopped me working." He gave women what he called, obviously for my benefit, "free-floating attention." I asked him, apropos of all this, what was wrong with having women in his mind, and he had replied with great irritation, "Well, you know what they're like!" I said that I didn't, and he suggested, quite reasonably, that perhaps I should find out.

One recurrent theme in the early sessions was his attitude of if-you-don't-know-then-I'm-not-going-to-tell-you. He gave me a prevailing impression that to ask a question of him was to expose myself as preposterously dim. He exuded an ethos in which to need anything—or to be seen to be wanting—was a sign of stupidity. When I put something of this to him, he said, "Well obviously, people only ask questions when there's something they don't know!" It was easy to imagine what it would be like to work for him; and I certainly didn't want to be one of his girlfriends. The currency here was exasperation. It was clear to me very quickly that he was bluffing out a disappointment. The configuration we kept finding ourselves in was an impasse between two polarized subjects—one dismissively contemptuous; one dismayed by his own inadequacy. The catastrophe my patient had to avert was the humiliation of a reversal happening. Once I realized that this man was living in a continual state of humiliation by an object—living unconsciously, as it were, the reversal of the pattern he sustained in the world—I began to feel a sense of impossibility. After all, to describe someone's humiliation is to humiliate that person. This, at least, was what I found myself thinking in his presence. Of course, this is what we do every day in psychoanalysis—find useful descriptions of humiliation. And yet with this man it was a stumbling-block thought. That one has ever been humiliated is humiliating. What did gradually occur to me, though, was that in this particular double act, this routine we had found for each other, both characters—the abject silly one and the brusque arrogant one—did in fact have something in common: a kind of shared secret, or rather shared interest, that kept them together. I say to him, "Why do you get up every morning and go to work?" He says, "Why do you think?" We are both utterly perplexed by the other's failed (or stalled) response. It is as though we have both told each other a really bad joke: we are both exasperated. In our very different ways we are both people who just don't get it.

After several weeks of this to-ing and fro-ing in which our respect for each other's tenacity increased along with our mutual frustration, he told me a good story about his mother. He arrived for the session, lay down on the couch, and said, "I suppose I should talk about my mother." I immediately thought, and just stopped myself saying, "Why is she important?" I gave an analytic *mmm*, and he started telling me about how much he loathed perfume. He had always hated his mother's perfume; he remembered her coming to kiss him goodnight, all dressed up to go out, "reeking," as he put it, of perfume; so much so that he had to "hide his nose" in the book he was reading in bed. This man, it should be said, has always been an avid reader. I said, "Maybe at that moment it was better to read than to desire her or feel jealous? You were hiding your penis in a book." And to my amazement he carried on as though we were having a conversation. "It seemed like a hint, to me." "What was she hinting about?" I asked, and he said, "I don't know why I said that; it wasn't a hint, it was a trick." I said, "What's the difference between a hint and a trick?" and he said, "There's no difference; they're the same thing." I said, "Trick makes me think either that someone is being fooled or that we are talking about prostitutes." He said to me, in the present tense, "Why does my mother have to go out?" It was a kind of enraged plea: the first moment between us of anything like regression, the first moment, that is, of heartfeltness. I said, "Your mother's perfume was her smell that you had to share with other people. When she wore perfume, she was hinting: about some exciting life of hers away from you." He said, becoming really boyish and megalomaniac, "Wouldn't it be great to invent a perfume that a lot of women loved and then to discontinue it." I said, "You mean to have some real control over how women smell?" And he agreed.

This chapter is about what kind of trick a hint is. About whether we can avoid ending up saying that all language is hinting, and so, for example, that we can end up where we prefer to begin, believing that there are two kinds of psychoanalytic communication—the patient associates and the analyst interprets—rather than, say, an entanglement of hints. For good and not so good reasons, we don't want to think of analysis—or even, perhaps, ordinary conversation—as mutual hinting. But my patient's example is, as it was for him, compelling. Language, one might say, is like perfume; it circulates to unpredictable effect. We might make our words smell as nice as they can, but they will go into the world and be made use of sometimes beyond our wildest intentions. They will fuel that dreamwork of everyday life called gossip. They will evoke idiosyncratic personal histories—what we call associations—in their listeners ("The ear says more / Than any tongue. / The ear sings better / Than any sounds / It hears on earth," the Scottish poet W. S. Graham writes in "The Hill of Intrusion"). Words are like perfume, and perfume is hinting. In some states of mind—in certain contexts—a hint will seem like a trick.

An emblem of what is at stake here is provided by the famous, funny example that Wittgenstein gives in his *Philosophical Investigations*. Why, he asks, when somebody points, do we look at what they are pointing at rather than looking up their arm? The answer, he says, is simple; we look at the object because we have learned a rule. People like us share this convention; our culture has taught us what the signs mean, where to look. We know how this works, and anyone who goes on looking up arms when something is being pointed out to them will never get anywhere.

Now hinting, of course, complicates this. A certain kind of psychoanalytic logic might say that when people are literally or metaphorically pointing, they unconsciously might want us to look up their arm. Their body must be more interesting than anything else they want to show us. So one question here is, what has to be done to pointing to make it hinting? We may think that the aim of interpretation is to work out—from the patient's associations—what he is pointing at. That either we want to show the patient that he is hinting, or what he might be hinting at, or both. But a hint, one could also say, is something another person can use; indeed, it is designed for use; even if it is a kind of test of the other person's capacity to use a communication (a hint can humiliate the other person, or free something in him; as a liminal concept it is a dare). It is in this sense the opposite of an order. It is the difference between my arriving at your house and saying "Get me a drink," and my arriving at your house and saying "It's very hot today." A lot of so-called good manners are orders disguised as hints. I want to suggest that there are two kinds of psychoanalytic interpretation. One kind aims to turn hints into orders; the other kind tries to turn orders into hints. Both are useful, but they make very different kinds of world. We might caricature this by wondering whether we want to turn the patient's romance into pornography, or his pornography into romance. (I think there is a serious question here about which is the most generous thing to do.) A hint may tantalize, but it also invites interpretation; indeed, at its best, it stimulates the object's capacity for thought and response. A hint might give the other person room (it may merely tantalize); an order is organized to confine him.

In psychoanalysis we know that the patient is hinting; what else could he be doing given the anguish of desire, the dreamwork, secondary revision, the repertoire of defenses. The analyst, of course, does not, cannot, exempt herself from these processes, but nevertheless it is assumed that in the process of reconstruction and interpretation the analyst is doing something other than free-associating. The analyst, just by virtue of using language, may not be able to avoid hinting—to escape ambiguity— but it is not, as it were, her job to hint. It is not her intention. So I want to use the idea of hinting to compare two styles of interpretation, and to wonder, by the same token, what the analyst committed to hinting would be up to. So I want to turn briefly now to another boy tricked by perfume—Richard, the young hero of Melanie Klein's fascinating *Narrative of a Child Analysis.*

III

Richard was a ten-year-old boy whom Melanie Klein treated for four months during the Second

World War. Richard, Klein tells us, was a disappointment to his mother. She preferred his elder brother, whom she had no need to worry about. But Richard, Klein writes,

> was an extremely difficult child to live with; he had no hobbies to occupy him, was over-anxious and over-affectionate towards his mother and, since he could not bear to be away from her, clung to her in a persistent and exhausting way, his hypochondriacal fears related to her health as well as his own.

The picture is of a very anxious child who could never quite make it into his mother's affections.

In the sixth session of the treatment, after some remarkable interpretative work in which the reader, or at least this reader, is as impressed as Richard was by Klein's sympathetic knowledge of him, Richard asks Klein what his mother had told her when arranging for his therapy. "Mrs K. gave a short report: mummy had mentioned his being often worried, his fear of children, and his other difficulties. She had also told Mrs. K. about him as a young child, including his operations." She is noticeably, and appropriately, both vague and brief. And it is in fact her analytic reticence that stimulates, as it should, his symbolic activity. She has hinted at a number of possibilities—as indeed do the few toys she sees as integral to her technique—and he tells her a story. Her minimum of detail prompts something in him; she tells him very little, and he tells her about his circumcision, when somebody took something away from him. When, at least as he experienced it, another woman, his mother, tricked him into a traumatic deprivation; he was robbed of something essential, a bit of his penis, knowledge of what really went on between his mother and Klein.

Of course, there are as many readings, as many interpretations, of sessions as there are readers and moments in time. In my reading of Richard's response to Klein's "short report," he is telling her, among other things, a parable about the analysis; about how people give him things and take them away:

> Richard was very pleased with this report, but it was clear that he was still doubtful and suspicious. He at once took up the story of his operations in great detail. He remembered something of his circumcision which took place when he was about three. He had no

pain, but it was awful being given ether. He had
been told beforehand that he would be given
some kind of perfume to smell and was
promised that nothing else would be done to
him (this tallied with his mother's account). He
took with him a bottle of perfume and wanted
them to use this instead of their perfume.
When this was not allowed, he wanted to throw
the bottle at the doctor, and even now he would
like to fight him. He had hated the doctor ever
since. He hated the smell of ether and was still
afraid of it. Suddenly he said, referring to the
moment when the ether was given: "It was as if
hundreds or thousands of people were there."
But he felt that his nurse was there with him
and that she would protect him.

He was told that he would be given some kind
of perfume—that was all that would happen; and it
wasn't true (it wasn't perfume, it was ether; and he
was circumcised). He was perhaps encouraged, but
certainly allowed, to take his own perfume—after
all, why be given someone else's if you have your
own—but of course he wasn't allowed to use it because his mother had lied to him. He had been
tricked by his mother even if it was, clearly, her at-

tempt to reassure him. It is striking that, at least in her account of the session, Klein does not mention the perfume; Richard tells her of two more operations in which it is the ether that traumatized him. Klein does not get, or ask for, any of his associations to perfume. The basic story is: you are forced to exchange your perfume for someone else's, and then you lose a bit of your penis. His perfume, his penis, and his preferences were effectively belittled. What goes on behind his back—whether it is Klein and his mother discussing him, or the doctor operating on him—is some trick to do with perfume. Some people's perfume—even if it is called ether—can be extremely dangerous and frightening. You don't know what people are using it to do to you.

Richard's mother had, unusually, brought him to the session because "he was too frightened of children to come by himself." So Richard had, in a sense, brought his own perfume to the session; but then he was given Klein's. So one of Richard's questions might have been, what kind of operation is analysis? How Klein actually interprets this material is entirely plausible:

> Mrs K. interpreted the strength of his feel-
> ings of persecution; he had said he felt sur-

rounded by hundreds and thousands of enemies, and quite powerless. He had only one
friend to protect him, the nurse *standing for* the
good mummy. But there was also in his mind
the bad mummy, his mother who had told him
a lie and therefore, he felt, had joined up with
his enemies. The bad doctor whom he wanted
to fight stood for the bad father who would
make him helpless and cut off his penis.

What I am interested in here is this (sexually suggestive) phrase that recurs throughout the interpretations she reports—indeed, throughout the case
history—of one thing "*standing for*" another. This,
one can say, is interpretation as pointing. She shows
or tells Richard that when he refers to the bad
doctor he is actually referring to, pointing at, the
bad, castrating father. She points at his words to tell
him what they are pointing at. Now pointing, as
Wittgenstein's example makes clear, depends upon
the acceptance of a convention. In this country—
let's call it Melanie Klein's consulting room—the
convention is that at this particular moment when
Richard talks about the kind nurse, he actually
means the good mummy. But Richard, of course,
may not have known about this convention, this rule,

until he met Mrs. Klein. Now Mrs. Klein might say, faced with this objection, that of course he knew because she is talking about some truth of the unconscious, or the way the internal world works. But then there is still the question of where or rather from whom she has acquired this knowledge. With whom has she learned this language—the kind of rhetoric required to make a privileged vocabulary? There is, one can see, a regression here into genealogy (the answer to these questions might be that she learned this from Ferenczi, Abraham, Freud, her children, and so on). But one way or another, orders have been passed down the line. To say that one thing stands for another is more akin to an order than a suggestion or a hint. It is no more nor less true—for who could arbitrate?—but it is a different way of proceeding. What is perfume or analysis for? To put you to sleep for your own benefit? It is powerful, and contagious. This perfume called ether tells you what to do. You can only submit to it, even if it is obviously in your best interests to do so. Perfume can be so disarming, so seductive, that you might want to know what's underneath it, so to speak. What, in Klein's language, we can't help wondering, does perfume stand for?

Interestingly, in her second note to the session—

and one of the many fascinating things about the *Narrative* is that Klein went on working on the notes virtually until her death—she writes:

> The accusation against the mother that, by causing sexual desires towards her, she is guilty not only of having aroused them but of having seduced the child, appears frequently in analysis. This accusation is rooted in the actual experience of having been physically touched and thereby stimulated. In some cases a certain amount of unconscious or even conscious seduction actually enters into the relation of the mother towards the child. Nevertheless, I think it is very important to take account of and analyse the projection of the child's own sexual desires on to the mother, and of his wish to seduce her.

Is sexual desire an order or a hint? Or to put it another way, where does it come from, the child or the mother? Perfume, let us say—certainly that perfume called ether—stands for something irresistible, something unavoidable, something that, in psychoanalytic terms, arouses our resistances because it cannot be resisted. What kind of perfume is psychoanalysis; perhaps Klein is wondering in this note not only where does sexuality come from—is the mother the cause or the reason?—but where does the unconscious come from in analysis, from the analyst or the patient? What we call the unconscious might be simply a description a person recognizes—feels a positive or negative affinity for—but that had apparently never occurred to him before. Perhaps Klein's work arouses such ferocious hostility in some people because she is doing something openly that analysts would prefer not to acknowledge that they all do— indeed, can't help doing—that is, make up the patient's unconscious. Show through persuasive description what the patient is unconsciously pointing at, what the words he uses stand for. The unconscious resides in its description. No interpretation, no unconscious.

Klein's note poses a very simple question: Who seduces whom? Does the mother seduce the child or the child the mother? Is sexuality the product of seduction or the source of it? And perhaps then in the same way, analysis can become a question of who seduces whom, or who produces the patient's unconscious, who produces the most compelling vocabulary (for what the patient affects not to know). As the four sentences of Klein's important note gain momentum, she moves firmly from the mother as the source of the child's desire—the mother as seductress—to the child as the source of the child's desire. The note, in other words, is a miniature history of psychoanalysis, the reworking of an earlier trauma to do with the seduction theory. "In some cases," she concludes, "a certain amount of unconscious or even conscious seduction actually enters into the relation of the mother toward the child. *Nevertheless, I think it is very important to take account of and analyse the child's projection of his own sexual desires on to the mother, and of his wish to seduce her* [my italics]." It would not be bizarre to think of this conclusion as a preemptive strike against the analyst's own self-doubt. As if she is thinking, "What if I the analyst am seducing the patient with my sublimated sexuality that is called psychoanalytic interpretation?" It is integral to Klein's method that the analyst is absolutely clear whose unconscious is being understood, whose unconscious is there to be described. The very definitiveness of her stance is, of course, a provocation. Assertions are a reaction formation against questions.

I want to suggest that hints muddle us up with other people; they are mutually and unpredictably implicating (I think of hints as the currency of what we call unconscious communication, our unavoidably being mixed up with each other). Orders, by contrast, involve a collusion that instates a difference. An order, in some fundamental sense, can only be accepted or rejected; it cannot, like a hint, be easily used. When Klein writes of one figure *standing for* another, she issues something akin to an instruction, or an order: that is really this. This, I think, is one of the many reasons that she is such an instructive figure in the history of psychoanalysis. She really confronts us—indeed continually struggles with—this fundamental question of where or who the unconscious comes from. What are the viable alternatives, if any, to seduction when two people talk to each other? It is her very stridency in these matters that is so impressive, unless we use her to intimidate ourselves.

For Klein, I think it is fair to say, a hint is a trick; and it is the trickiness of certain parts of the self that are so debilitating. We can think here, for example, of her preoccupation with the subtle ingenuities of envy, the sophisticated insinuation of the death instinct into the personality: what Freud called its silence. Winnicott, one could say, by way of drama-

tizing an old contrast, is all hinting; he is almost phobic about telling anyone what to do, and no less coercive, of course, as a consequence. If Klein, at least
to her critics, errs on the side of instructing the patient—telling him what he means—Winnicott errs
on the side of being suggestive (his critics might say
he errs on the side of being cute, but calls it playing).
What is Winnicott's squiggle game if not a hint to
the patient? The famous spatulas on Winnicott's
desk were put there as a temptation staged for the
child.[5] Winnicott claims that he only starts "teaching" in analysis when he is "very tired." Klein's critique of Anna Freud was that by exploiting the
child's positive transference, by encouraging the
child's identification with the analyst, she was merely
"teaching" the child instinct control, not reaching, as
Klein was, the depths of the child's personality. In
other words, for both Klein and Winnicott the
teacher—after the seducer—is the analyst's negative
ideal. It is teaching and seduction—two activities
that seem inextricable—that Klein and Winnicott
want to distinguish from what they themselves do in
psychoanalysis. And yet when Freud famously referred to analysis as an "after-education," he seemed
to be implying that we need not be afraid of learning

a thing or two in analysis—indeed, being taught something about ourselves by the analyst. Or to put it another way, that what we call learning needn't stop in analysis even if it is not always clear who or what is doing the teaching: or even what learning itself is. I want to suggest that analysis—unlike teaching and seduction—is an education through hinting, about hinting. That hinting, if you like, is a kind of go-between between teaching and seduction, sustaining both a complicity and a difference. The best kind of teaching, like the worst kind of seduction, is all hinting. For some people it would be the other way around.

When Marion Milner was experimenting with what she called "free drawing" as a kind of visual equivalent of free association, she found, as she writes in *On Not Being Able to Paint*, that the useless doodles were "the kind in which a scribble turned into a recognizable object too soon":

> It seemed almost as if, at these moments, one could not bear the chaos and uncertainty about what was emerging long enough, as if one had to turn the scribble into some recognizable whole when in fact the thought or

mood seeking expression had not yet reached that stage. And the result was a sense of false certainty, a compulsive and deceptive sanity, a tyrannical victory of the common sense view which always sees objects as objects, but at the cost of something else which was seeking recognition, something that was more to do with imaginative than with common sense reality.

What Milner suggests here is that there is some essential complicity, or link, between a hunger for recognizable objects and what she calls a "sense of false certainty, a compulsive and deceptive sanity." There is the tyranny, that is to say, of a cramping internal ideal, an aspiration toward the obvious. Like the child learning to talk, or beginning to find his feet in language, there is an inevitable pressure—both internal and external—to make something easily sharable, to produce the consensual object—the acceptable phrase, the reassuring drawing—rather than the ambiguous or enigmatic object. When this happens, the hint—the risk of what's possible—is turned into an order. Fear of the unknown is cured through flight into the intelligible. The new—what Milner refers to as the as yet indeterminate "thought or mood seeking expression"—is preempted. The familiar, the unsurprising, restores our collusive sanity.

IV

Hints—including the hints we give ourselves, like Milner's doodles—can be made something of; orders can only be submitted to or rejected. Milner's example suggests that it is as though we are continually giving ourselves orders, trying to live up to coercive inner ideals. Conforming, out of fear, with what too quickly makes sense, our hunger for recognition becomes a self-blinding. Eager to shore up a sensible world with overfamiliar objects, we are ruthlessly loyal to what we already know, to the past, or rather, to our always spurious omniscience about the past that allows us to treat it as the world we know (the family was never full of people we knew, it was just where we started knowing people). As though it were full of recognizable objects, as though consensual reality was sane enough to keep us safe, or vice versa.

But Milner's fable about the fate of curiosity has an irony built into it that is akin to the irony of orders. It implies that there is such a thing as a (wholly) recognizable object, just as an order implies, reassures us, that in the giving and carrying out of an order we can know what we are saying and doing (orders as the ultimate proof that there is no unconscious). To treat an order, or any kind of rule or instruction, as merely suggestive—to turn it into something a little more to one's taste—is to radically revise the nature of authority (obedience would be merely fear of interpretation). It is to acknowledge— as psychoanalysis does with the notion of the unconscious and its dreamwork—the impossibility and therefore the violence of all forms of sovereignty ("Sovereignty," Jean Elshtain writes, "as task and tale . . . invites a disdain for life itself"). If I accuse you of distorting what I have said to you, it implies that I am the absolute authority on the meaning of my words (it implies you have no interpretative freedom and that I have no unconscious). If I regard your, indeed my, doodle as silly because I can't see what it is, it implies that I am the absolute authority on recognition of what is plausible, or even viable. All such aesthetic criteria are criteria of what is considered possible. At their worst they predict the future by preempting it. But then rules are always made for a future that can never be known. And it is this, of course, that makes all modern forms of moral prescription so complicated. Our personal morality, our

moral vocabulary, is designed for situations it may
never have dreamed of. It averts what Milner calls
"chaos and uncertainty" by flight into familiar—
literally old-fashioned—precept. Living by the rules
is another way of hoping that the future will be like
the past.

Milner's fable about curiosity, in other words, is
also a fable about morality, about the relationship
between what once might have been called wonder
(curiosity and its spin-offs, amazement and awe) and
our moral ideals. If curiosity, and what I am calling
interest, is always in the service of the new, of the
old renewed, then it is always revisionary, making fu-
tures out of the past, turning orders into hints and
following them up, these orders being both the instructions involved in growing up and their source in
the available traditions and canons the culture pro-
vides.

But in what sense can the child do with the moral
facts of life—the morality she both inherits and is
taught—what Freud says she does with the biological
facts of life? Since all sexual theories are moral
theories—stories about what it is possible and/or acceptable for people to do—the child in her sexual
researches is also evolving what might seem like a
contradiction in terms: a personal morality—a

morality designed according to the developmental needs of the moment (so, if we are Freudians, we can talk about oral morality, anal morality, and so on). It is a morality, by the same token, that might include—rather than merely grow out of—each of its evolving stages. So a person's private morality, unlike his official morality, is a coincidence—a virtual melee—of different periods in his life.

Depending on the ethos in which the child is brought up, he will be more or less morally curious, having been more or less encouraged, consciously and unconsciously by the adults, to treat morality as an order or a hint, as a recognizable (already formed) whole, or as something, like a child, in a process of evolution. He may be able or allowed to notice, for example, that the voice urging him to be nice is itself not very nice, is indeed cruel in its demands, or that being bad in one situation is being good in another, or that moral ideals are as mortal, as transient, as the people who make them. He may notice, as an adolescent, that the more morality oversimplifies, the harsher and more intimidating it becomes; that the numinous thing is to simplify the moral life. What psychoanalysis describes as the modifying of the superego brings with it this idea that morality is subject to innovation, that where superego was, there ego can be (it is as though the superego as both moralistic tyrant and guardian of one's cherished ideals has to be reminded that it is not omniscient, that sovereignty debauches). The child is all the time improvising her own morality through curiosity and dream, and having it imposed upon her in the necessary process of adaptation through identification with the character ideals of the culture, mediated by the parents. The child has foisted upon her the culture's repertoire of acceptable ways of being and answers back, often in rage, but more acceptably in inventiveness and innovation.

The child's freedom, the child's self-fashioning project, depends upon her being able to treat orders and instructions as though they were also hints and suggestions, as open invitations rather than merely prescriptions. Rules are not merely abided by, they are also sounded out; they require that unfounded competence called guesswork. But this means that the child, as she edges her way into this, is always caught in a complicated clash of internal ideals (there is the wish for competence and the something-to-be-mourned in its acquisition). Put crudely, there is the necessary ideal of adaptation, of becoming one way or another a good person by the standards of the tribe. And this entails assuming the characteristics—honesty, hygiene, competitiveness—that allow the child to keep in touch (the analyst John Rickman once said that being mad was when you couldn't find anyone who could stand you).

It is a paradox of some interest that nurture always involves compliance; the child must submit to the fact that some things are too hot to touch, that the parents have a history, and so on. But joining the group is not solely a matter of forced agreements; the child, like the psychoanalyst, also undoes and recombines the connections the culture wants her to make (you handle it because it's too hot to handle). So the ideal of adaptation is always matched—at least in posttraditional societies—by the ideal of improvisation: the child and the adult's relative freedom to transform, according to their unconscious desire, the cultural givens. This often involves changing the game rather than merely changing the rules (the importance of one thing replaces the importance of another, and those who like the new thing call it progress). So there is what might be called a commonsense struggle for survival, and a struggle for the survival of imaginative vision. In psychoanalytic terms this would be called the wish and whatever comes to meet it. For Freud, part of the legacy of childhood was an exorbitant sense of the possibilities for satisfaction and so of the exorbitant moral ideals required to temper them (otherwise called the resolution of the Oedipus complex, the sufficient internalization of parental prohibitions). We live as if the world were made for us, and as if it were made for someone else, who knows nothing about us. We live as if we know exactly what life is like, in satisfaction—and then notice (to put it mildly) how our wishing works. But to believe that the world is, or could be, as we want it to be—lived as irony or without irony; that is, lived as comedy or tragedy—is the precondition of the child's life. That is what is in the beginning—the Promise, not the Word. The child, in other words, does not suffer from a lack of commitment. Tantrums are only for the engaged.

It may be more interesting that things begin at all than that they continue or even end (we can mourn for what is lost, but what can we do with what is added on?). The hint, taken or given, is a form of hope. Expecting the earth, we get something.

part four

JUST RAGE

The facts of life do not penetrate to the sphere
in which our beliefs are cherished; they did not
engender those beliefs, and they are powerless
to destroy them.

—PROUST, *Swann's Way*

I

We wouldn't think of anything as a tragedy if we did not have a deeply ingrained sense of order already there to be affronted. Tragedy in life, and as art—not to mention the minor tragedies of everyday life: the insults, the accidents, the obstacles that are the occasion of our daily melodramas or irritation—exposes by violation our mostly unconscious assumptions about how the world should be; and how often we take it for granted that it is as it should be (a world, say, without our death already in it). Our rage when we lose our keys—whatever it discloses by way of personal meaning or internal division—shows us that we also live in a world in which keys are always to hand.

There is a world elsewhere of fluent, uninterrupted competence, a world in which everything works (the trains run on time). A world in which we need never feel anger or, rather, the unbearable conflict that we use anger to abolish, to void ourselves of (we don't want to kill the person we hate most, the psychoanalyst Ernest Jones once remarked; we want to kill the person who creates in

us the most intolerable conflict). There is no anger
that is not revenge, no rage without the betrayal of
an ideal, however unconscious, however exorbitant
that ideal might be. In my bad temper I expose not
merely my loss of control—that so-much-wished-for
transgression—but far more shamefully I expose
my furtive utopianism, my horrifying, passionate
ideal of, and for, myself. In other words, I am humiliated at that moment when I can no longer bear—
that is, rationalize—the disparity between who I
seem to be and who I want to be; when, in psychoanalytic language, the gap between my ego and my
ego-ideal becomes irretrievable. The one person I
can never mourn the loss of is my ideal self. Anything, even the shameful excitement of humiliation,
is better than that.

If anger is evidence of our idealism, our self-
idealization—of just how unconscious, how frantic
our sense of justice is—it also reveals, by the same
token, that our potential for humiliation is the root of
morality. It is indeed curious how impressed we are
by being diminished, how vulnerable we always are
to slight and ridicule (as though we are, somewhere,
always already ironized in our own eyes; as though,
from one point of view, all our claims are boasts).
Nothing confirms more clearly the impossibility of

amorality—our embeddedness in a moral world—than our capacity to be humiliated. That we can feel humiliated reveals how much what matters to us matters to us. Our rage is itself a commitment to something, to something preferred. Indeed, how would a person immune from, or ignorant of, humiliation know what a good life was? Our betrayals, our travesties that issue in anger— our losing of keys—are forms of awkward, untimely revelation.

It is as though our morality, as disclosed by our anger, is a kind of private madness, a secret personal religion of cherished values that we only discover, if at all, when they are violated. The virtues we can consciously formulate and try to abide by are, one might say, our official morality. Our unofficial, more idiosyncratic morality is only available, so to speak, through humiliation. Once you know who or what humiliates you, you know what it is about yourself that you ultimately value, that you worship. Tell me what makes you enraged—what makes you feel truly diminished—and I will tell you what you believe or what you want to believe about yourself. What, that is, you imagine you need to protect to sustain your love of life.

If I say, look at the wind in the trees, all you can *see* is the trees, moving in their way. If we want to

look at our private—and often all-too-public—
morality, what we can often see and hear and feel is
our rage. It is from our discontents that we can infer
our ideals. What Freud tried to persuade us of was
the extent to which, because we are driven by instinct—that is, his fiction of what instinct entailed—
we are therefore driven by ideals. It was hardly a
revelation in modern Europe that sexuality was a
powerful force in people's lives (Freud did not discover sexuality; he discovered how sexuality resists
articulation); it was, perhaps, more surprising that
we could describe our morality as one form our sexuality can take. We can, for example, imagine the
idea of neither justice nor sexual perversion without
the idea of judgment. In other words, from a psychoanalytic point of view, our ideals are like objects
of desire; indeed, they are objects of desire that have
been sublimated, redescribed in more acceptable
form (it might sound better to want to be a bad person than to want to be married to your mother). It is
easy to see both how and why our ideals for ourselves—to be good, to be bad, to be successful, to be
just—can become more compelling to us than other
people. People are more difficult, and more satisfy-
ing, to love than ideals. And our ideals create the illu-

sion that we can stop time, that something is perma-
nent even if we are falling short.

II

Anger, then, is only for the engaged; for those
with projects that matter (not the indifferent, the in-
souciant, the depressed). That is to say, those for
whom something has gone wrong but who "know,"
in their rage, that it could be otherwise. Whether
from inside through the silent working of a putative
death instinct, or from outside through the always
frustrating other who never gives us enough of
something or other, there is a rupture. At its most
minimal our picture is of something interrupted, an
epiphany of obstacles. Of a creature unavoidably
deflected from its aim (of satisfaction, of justice, of
mastery, of "more life," of dying in its own way).
Our rage speaks of intrusion and sabotage and betrayal, but also, paradoxically, of insistence and refusal and hope. It is, in other words, inextricable
from revenge. Indeed, can we imagine an anger that
is not vengeful, even though it often needs to con-
ceal—to displace—its object?

Our angers are inarticulate theories of justice; they are articulated, acted out, in revenge. Revenge, one might say, is the genre of rage. ("What," patients always ask from the couch, "can I do with my rage? What am I supposed to do with it?" "What," one could ask in reply, "would be a possible answer?") If rage renders us helpless, revenge gives us something to do. It organizes our disarray. It is one way of making the world, or one's life, make sense. Revenge turns rupture into story. And it shows us the extent to which meaning is complicit with the possibility of redress, with a belief that losses can be made good (revenge as savagely optimistic mourning). Because tragedy always threatens to baffle the possibility of action—our minor tragedies, that is to say, as well as real ones—revenge keeps hope alive.

Real tragedy questions our capacity—our wish— to make meaning; revenge preempts the question. The revenger is purpose incarnate. Unless he is Hamlet, he knows both that something can be done and what to do. Indeed, the idea of revenge makes Hamlet wonder whether his life is worth living; that is what is so extraordinary about Hamlet. But the average revenger, once he has been injured, knows what his life is for; he knows what interests him. For him a wound is like a pure gift of meaning, a vocation. For the revenger the only question is how. A terrible optimist, he believes in justice, in both its possibility and its value. Because he (now) knows what he wants, he knows what his life means. And yet it is precisely the redemptive nature of revenge— its implicit belief in making good, or getting even— that might make us wonder about humiliation itself, about how prone we are to rage. The rage that at once protests our extreme vulnerability and asserts our refusal to submit.

III

What, to put it starkly, is humiliation? What is there to be enraged about? Or indeed, for what is rage the only available solution, the only self-cure? The answer to these questions confronts us—at both a personal and a political level—with the relationship between justice and resourcelessness. In other words, with the provenance of our sense of entitlement. It is, ironically, from my rage that I can reconstruct what I take to be my rights. And there is, as everyone knows, an uneasy tension between the so-called rights of man and the individual's always recondite, unconscious sense of what he is due. I am secretly privileged: I have needs that I think of as my rights; my life is ritualized prestige. And yet I am one among others. As every child soon notices, however important he is—however beautiful or loved or clever—he is also nothing special. There is always a point of view—that will forever haunt him—from which he is of no interest (this is the power of the primal scene; in the glare of the parents' sexual relationship, the child is not important). It is a point of view, a blank stare, that can only enrage him and in which he must continually reconstitute himself; what we call narcissism is the (hopeless) attempt to abolish this point of view, which is incarnated for us most vividly by the figure of the depressed or the sexual parent. In rage we make our presence felt, if only to ourselves. Our excitement is like a reminder, a sign of life. Or a hope that we can redress the searing humiliation of being ignored when we are in need of something.

Humiliation is always a game played with hope. It turns wishing into a form of persecution. We may be the animals who can make promises, but we are also, by the same token, the animals who humiliate, who are so adept at destroying hope, the animals who can take so much pleasure in diminishing ourselves and others. It is as though humiliation—exclusion, betrayal, violation, combining as it does our abjection and our grandiosity—is one of our fundamental pictures of what people can do together. The humiliation scene itself is like a recurring and primal bad dream, the unavoidable link between private and political life (humiliation as the hard currency of oppression). To humiliate someone is to make oneself unforgettable, a malign way of keeping a place in someone's mind (the ethical project of psychoanalysis is to diminish humiliation, to find an alternative to sadomasochism as a model for human relations). And so, integral to humiliation, its guarantor, is tantalization, the promise that may always only be promising. The promise that, by definition, can always be false, that keeps our wishing up in the air. It is, of course, only possible to humiliate someone because they have some hope. Only those people who have a future can be tantalized.

To humiliate someone you have to exploit their dependence on you. First you must establish it, then you use it (to secure certain essentials for yourself by instilling fear in the other). You create or satisfy a need in the other; then you make him ashamed, or guilty, or fearful of it (the need for recognition, for desire, for safety, for something again deemed essential). This is a description—albeit excessively malign,

if not starkly sadomasochistic—of every child's experience at the hands of his parents. It is a description of the Oedipus complex. It is humiliating that
the only people who can satisfy your desire from
your point of view won't, and from their point of
view can't.

The parents may be everything to the child, but
the child can never be everything to the parents (sustaining the illusion that the child *can* be everything to
the parents creates psychic havoc). There is an inevitable element of humiliation in simply being a
child, though the child's relative helplessness can be
more or less exploited by the parents; the child is not
sufficient unto himself, he cannot bring himself up.
We have, then, humiliation as the tyranny of one's
need for the other. Or rather, one's inevitable need
experienced as—or turned into—a tyranny. And yet
a moment's thought will tell us that it is not the need
that is tyrannical but the fantasy of self-sufficiency. If
I am, know, and have everything, then wanting is literally inconceivable ("Everything is nothing," as
Morton Densher says in Henry James's *The Wings of
the Dove*). We are enraged because we live as though
everything is already there, and is already always
ours. So our rage is an elegy, a frenzied nostalgia, for
something that never existed. For something that

could never exist. Who is the more dependent, after all—a god or his creation?

If we describe ourselves as living, at least at the very beginning, as though we control the resources—the mother, as Winnicott says, fitting in with the infant's omnipotence to sustain the illusion that she is his creation—then what we call rage might be the first stage of some process of enlightenment. The dispelling of a primal illusion. The simple and clearly avoidable acknowledgment that there are other people in the world; the celebration of our transience. Rage as our first tribute to otherness, both the otherness within and the otherness without. And yet, we can only ironize, but never, apparently, dissolve the grandiosity of our sense of entitlement. But then if we lost our rage, we would lose our link to childhood, to those beginnings we now hold as sacred in the absence of a god. We may be childlike in our sexuality, but we are truly infantile in our rage.

IV

In one sense it is a perverse loyalty to ourselves— or rather to one version of ourselves, an idealized or preferred one—that makes humiliation possible.

We will humiliate or be humiliated—and from a psychoanalytic point of view, we always do both, unconsciously identifying with the position we disown—when our personal gods are profaned; that is, when our often unconscious values and ideals are insulted or under threat. Men in this culture often abuse women when their masculinity feels compromised, and women often return to those dangerous relationships when the redemptive power of their love is in question. Children, not surprisingly, are often spiteful over issues of privilege and entitlement. Rage becomes the often forlorn hope of reinstating a damaged ideal version of ourselves—not exactly making our presence felt, but keeping whatever we value most about ourselves in circulation. From a psychoanalytic point of view, growing up entails loss of status—a kind of disembodying—and then its attempted restoration. And what loses status above all in the process of growing up is the desires of childhood. In other words, Freud presents us with an ironic progress myth: We want to be what we are already. In our rage we are demanding that something be returned to us; or that it be destroyed because it tantalizes us with hope.

The various hobbyhorses of contemporary psychoanalysis—myths of development, the perverse romance of "emotional nurture," the fetishization of language, the obsession with "relationship"—all of them in their different ways drift toward a disavowal of the sensuous pleasures of childhood. In their commitment to the child's future they forget his bodily beginnings. After Freud (and Ferenczi) psychoanalytic stories about childhood become stories about how to get out: phobic about infantile sexuality and the child's interest in bodies (in child sexual abuse this returns in reverse—the adult overly interested in the child's body). But what was radically puzzling originally about Freud's work was the implication that, in one sense, after childhood there was nowhere to go, and that the disillusionments of the Oedipus complex were an acknowledgment of this. You couldn't marry your mother or father, but the erotic life evolved in the crucible of those first passionate relationships was an irresistible ideal. It could never be dispensed with, only (hopefully) displaced or deferred. And even before such Oedipal crises dawn, the infant and young child is immersed in the best of all possible worlds. Freud was asserting, Norman O. Brown wrote nearly forty years ago in *Life Against Death,* that in spite of two thousand years of higher education based on the notion that man is essentially a soul for mysterious accidental reasons imprisoned in a body, man remains incurably obtuse and still secretly thinks of himself as first and foremost a body. Our repressed desires are not just for delight, but specifically for delight in the fulfillment of the life of our own bodies. Children, at the stage of early infancy which Freud thinks critical, are unable to distinguish between their souls and their bodies; in Freudian terminology, they are their own ideal. . . . Freud of course neither advocates nor thinks possible a return to a state of innocence; he is simply saying that childhood remains man's indestructible goal.

Freud is not saying that we are really children, but that the sensual intensities of childhood cannot be abolished, that our ideals are transformed versions of childhood pleasures. That the values and ambitions—the representations—of the adult are an obscured picture of the passions and conflicts and curiosities of childhood. (So the wish to be rich, for example, becomes a fantasy of uninhibited access, or of being exempt from dependent need.) Looking for-

ward, as Brown spells out, is a paradoxical form of
looking back. The future is where one retrieves the
pleasures, the bodily pleasures of the past. And to be
distracted from one's preoccupations as a child (and
as an adult), Freud intimates, is a subtle and insidious
form of humiliation. As the rages of childhood make
rather vivid—the frantic perplexity of adults faced
with the child's tantrum points up this dilemma—
compliance is always experienced by the child as de-
meaning (sadomasochism is the trick by which adults
make compliance and domination bearable by making them sexually exciting). But how could we possibly imagine a childhood that did not involve an
inevitable clash of needs between "his majesty the
baby" and the adults who care for him? How could
growing up be anything but an adaptation to something other than oneself, and therefore a disillusionment? The older word "struggle"—the struggle for
feeling and expression—might be more useful in this
context than the limiting biologism of "adaptation";
but nevertheless, the infant has to be initiated into
her culture.

All forms of parenting—like all forms of psychoanalysis—adapt the child and the patient to something. Fundamental forms of agreement are required between people of different status. If the

analyst believes the patient is in actuality a so-called decentered subject, then the analyst must persuade the patient that this is so, that his life will be better if he believes this. If the parent believes the child is, in actuality, in a state of original sin, then the parent must do what she can to convince the child of this and of the consequent value of attempts at goodness. (Humiliation turns up when the child consciously or unconsciously believes something that the adult needs him not to.) The child lives as if, say, his mother is a part of his body, or his sibling is an alien from Mars. The parents disabuse the child of these disruptive convictions, but the child, in Freud's view, goes on believing both things, indeed lives in a state of conflicting vocabularies as he struggles to secure his survival without too much cost to his pleasure. Freud's story about childhood is persuading us to value the conflict, to acknowledge that every point of view is true from its own point of view (psychoanalysis is the art of keeping the contradictions going). And if we emphasize the infantile sexuality of the child, as Freud did—the child's erotic apprehension of reality that is akin, as Brown suggests, to Blake's notion of vision—this has consequences for the ways in which we then imagine the project of a life. Every story about origins is a prediction about the past that becomes a covert prediction of the future.

We need to revive one stark version of Freud's story: There is a part of ourselves that adapts and a part of ourselves that doesn't. The part of ourselves that doesn't is not beyond culture, in Lionel Trilling's phrase, because it can only be described in the language of the culture. Freud calls the part that doesn't, variously, infantile sexuality, polymorphous perversity, the unconscious, the dreamwork, the death instinct, the id. He calls the part that does, the ego, and the part that does and doesn't, the superego. So we are not in and out of culture, but we are in culture in conflicting and contradictory ways. We do not suffer from conflict, Freud implies, we suffer from being able to bear too little conflict. From not being keen, in the poet and essayist William Empson's wonderful phrase, to "straddle the contradictions": to keep all the voices in play, to sustain the drama by stopping it from turning into a perpetual soliloquy.

In the various slights of everyday life it is as if we are treated with insufficient regard, not taken seriously enough, not believed, not desired, not noticed, not loved enough (the word "slight" itself, as part of the extensive vocabulary of belittlement, takes us just that bit closer to invisibility, to being a child).

And our reactions to these common slights expose with a terrible lucidity our mostly unconscious assumptions about our place in the world. Growing up, in other words, is not so much acquiring a more realistic sense of ourselves, but rather the process of forgetting our earliest entitlements, the body needs that turned to words (what Winnicott once referred to as "the imaginative elaboration of physical function"). In this sense we are the ways in which our bodies respond to culture.

It is now a commonplace assumption that something essential is lost, or at least attenuated, in the process of growing up. Whether it is called vision or imagination or vitality or hope, lives are considered to erode over time (the idealization of childhood and adolescence is reactive to this belief). And it is of course integral to this story to conceive of death as an enemy—as something we fight, something that makes surprise attacks—and not of a piece with our lives. At its most insidiously compliant, psychoanalysis has merely reinforced—through quasi-scientific redescription—these traditional stories: psychanalysis as the high art of disillusionment; the modern mythology of enlightened frustration, the comforting ironization of desire.

And yet by making bodily appetite, and therefore

imagination, the hero and heroine of his story, Freud was also, as it were, pushing us toward pleasure, trying to persuade us about the persuasions of the body: how the body performs its nonconformism (in symptoms, in jokes, in dreams, in error) throughout life. What Freud called dreamwork—and what modern pragmatism calls redescription—was a continual transfiguring of the facts of life by the fantasies of life. And this secret work that the individual was engaged in throughout life—this excess of wishing that makes history, this insistent, fantastic revision—was done to one end: to keep life worth living, to disclose not merely what can sustain us but what can transport us (in its avoidance of the ecstasies, psychoanalysis has sold its birthright for a mess of well-being). Our wishes, Freud intimates, are inspiring whether or not they are conducive to our happiness; and if our wishes don't make us happy, nothing else will. This was the enigma that Freud tried to formulate. We are only alive because we want, and yet it is in our wanting that we are obscure to ourselves. We believe in satisfaction, but we don't believe in conflict. As we grow up, we become the sophisticated antagonists of our own pleasure.

If our wanting and our self-knowledge are as radically at odds with each other as psychoanalysis itself suggests—and as they are, by definition, in child-hood—then psychoanalysis is indeed the symptom that purports to be the cure. By promoting poor sub-stitutes for satisfaction—by making sublimation such an ambitious, conceited story—it can covertly en-courage a loss of confidence in pleasure itself. Forgetting, in other words, that pleasure always be-gins and ends with the body and its inevitable, en-livening, enduring conflicts. And it can forget the child's ingenious love of life. If growing up did not mean growing out of things but growing into them again and again, our good life stories would have to change their shape. We would be answerable in quite different ways.

Coda

"Anthropologists," the sociologist Anthony Giddens has written, "used to deal with individuals and groups who by and large didn't answer back." It would indeed be strange if this were true of psychoanalysts. Psychoanalysis, one would like to think, as a form of treatment is about the possibilities of answering back; about analyzing the obstacles to replying, with a view to the patient ultimately speaking without fear of punishment (free association, one might say, is the reply that dare not speak its name). And Freud's theory of psychoanalysis seems to be about sexuality as both the conventional and the subversive way the individual answers back in, and to, culture. What Freud called the unconscious was like a repertoire of more or less illicit responses to being born, called desires, the dream itself a response of radical "crazy" redescription, the unconscious a forbidden kind of work. The Freudian child embarking on her sexual researches, with which this book started, never takes the facts of life lying down.

Freud's early case histories, the *Studies in Hysteria*, were artful stories about how certain women an-

swered back in families—and in the wider culture
that is the medium for the family—which preferred
them not to. Freud's newfound psychoanalytic
method encouraged them to answer back in words,
which were considered to be the more effective currency, rather than in physical symptoms (symptoms
are ways of answering back that obscure the demand). All this seemed sensible enough until it
dawned on Freud that the patient unconsciously
used the psychoanalytic setting to re-create the initial
traumatic scenario. In so far as the analyst was
merely a stooge, a stand-in for the original parent,
the patient might be persuaded to respeak without
fear of punishment. But the analyst, as Freud found
to his cost, could never be experienced by the patient
as exclusively just a substitute. Indeed, the whole
notion of transference only made sense if there
was something that wasn't transference. So then the
question arose: In what sense could the patient answer the analyst back as one adult to another? Did
psychoanalysis merely solve one problem in order to
re-create a similar one? After all, if the analyst places
himself beyond real criticism, he must fear it. Why is
separation the only thing the patient and the analyst
can do, once the transference has been "resolved"?

Psychoanalysis, in this sense, invites a demand in

order to refuse it, as though it were a cure by tantalization. "To urge the patient to suppress, renounce
or sublimate her instincts the moment she has admit-
ted her erotic transference would be not an analyti-
cal way of dealing with them but a senseless one,"
Freud writes in "Observations on Transference
Love," ". . . the patient will feel only humiliation,
and she will not fail to take her revenge for it." The
patient, in other words, is encouraged to (re)experi-
ence a rebuff, to undergo, in order to understand, a
terrible narcissistic wound. The patient loves and desires the analyst, and the only thing that is going to
happen is that it will be described (linked to the past),
but in the service, of course, of a better future life.
Once again, as in childhood, the patient is being told
the facts of life, the Oedipal facts of life.

In this case the facts of life, as theory, have a plausible ring to them (if they didn't, no one would ever
believe them). "Transference-love," Freud writes,
"has perhaps a degree less of freedom than the love
which appears in ordinary life and is called normal;
it displays its dependence on the infantile pattern
more clearly and is less adaptable and capable of
modification." From this point of view, anything that
is not subject to transformation—anything that pre-
cludes the work of change being done on it—is a

trauma. It stops time by sabotaging invention. It forecloses improvisation. The infantile love that is transference love is a problem because it protects us from the shock of the new; indeed, it makes the category of the new, or the unpredictable, redundant. Everybody becomes either a member of our original family or a version of ourselves. In our best redescriptions the present answers back to the past with a view to making a future (this happens, in spite of us, in our dreams). "Loyalty and intelligence," W. H. Auden once wrote, "are mutually hostile"; to acknowledge the new—to surprise oneself—is an infidelity, a betrayal of one's past.

So, does the patient love the analyst—or indeed anyone—only as a substitute, because they remind them of someone they once did love? Freud confronted this issue of the relationship between people's perception of each other and their invention of each other with a contradictory answer. We love people because they remind us of our earliest passions for our parents and ourselves; and we can only fully love them if we can recognize them as sufficiently different, as other. It is the difference between what I've been calling in this book an improvisation and a compulsion, a hint or an order, curiosity and habit. We can only have an erotic life by answering our parents back, by revising what they asked us, and what they asked of us.

But to what extent can we answer back to our theories about all these things? Just as some books, one might say, are more hospitable to interpretation—and some readers keener than others to make books their own—so some psychoanalytic (and other) forms of theory can seem to resist revision. It is an inevitability of some interest that the more deterministic the theory is, the more recalcitrant it is to individual innovation. Freudianism and Darwinism, for example, both see the individual as caught between two forms of instruction. For Freud the individual's ego struggles between the imperatives of the id and the imperatives of the external world, of the culture. For Darwinism there is natural selection and genetics. As a consequence of this, both stories, at their most reductive, make of morality a more or less sophisticated form of opportunism (both stories stress how much people's lives matter to them and how little they can do to sustain them). Morals become something between a talent for, and a trick of, survival—the survival of reproduction and the survival of pleasure. The individual is inventive but only within an already known horizon. The project is only too clear. We are doing what we are supposed

to be doing. We can't help it. We are being told what
to do by being told what we are in fact doing (living
our desire, reproducing our genes). We simply per-
form the essences that have been assigned to us. As
though our lives have already been organized for us,
and all we have to do is live them. We are condemned to hand ourselves over to some predesigned
purpose or other.

All the attempts to ascribe an essence to human
nature are ways of giving people a project, giving a
shape to their lives: that is their value. The psychoanalytic idea, for example—with its all too venerable
theological history—that a person's life is a war between his life instincts and his death instincts, pro-
vides a guideline for what might otherwise seem a
bewildering endeavor. Essences are what we can add
to appearances to make them weighty, to give them
sufficient gravity. But they can make us wonder, by
the same token, why we need to imagine that something is hidden—an unconscious instinctual life,
say—in order to make what we can see more interesting (the hidden can also be a cover story for what
is there to be seen); and why we prefer deterministic
theories in the first place.

The paradox of all the deterministic theories is
that they can only be discovered through the deter-

minisms they describe: God reveals God to us; our genes make us Darwinians (or geneticists); our desire produces psychoanalytic theory. They are closed systems—self-fulfilling prophecies—because they can both explain and include everything that might falsify them. In the terms of these theories we have to assume that every culture that knows nothing of genetics is still in the dark, that any individual who does not conceive of himself and his life as a war between a life and a death instinct is self-deceiving. In Darwin and Freud local knowledge becomes universal truth, as though the local was not sufficient and truth was what we really wanted. And two culturally and historically specific stories become "models," as though people were merely programmed by systems of belief, acting them out like scripts.

Deterministic theories like these—in which it is as if we are given orders by something or other (the unconscious, culture, DNA)—are always ironic in their effect because they can, at least in a secular society, only be made up by people, though they can seem—through their rhetorical strategies working within the culture's ruling conventions about truth—instructions from Reality. Or simply stories about the way the world is—Just-This stories (in science it is as though the world is finally speaking for itself, telling us what it's really like). And we can privilege what we say by claiming it comes from a superior source that we, or some of us, have unique access to—God, the tradition, the unconscious, scientific method. If we want to imagine an alternative to this, in old-fashioned language, we would have to imagine a local God who didn't lay down laws but simply made suggestions. What Nietzsche grandly called "the innocence of becoming"—the haphazard, unaccountable, intent project of a life—has been waylaid by the number of designs for a life on offer from those in the know!

By definition, of course, it doesn't make sense for us to think we can choose not to believe in such deterministic theories. Or at least if we do, we may have to become like Dostoevsky's Underground Man, staking our claim on two plus two equaling five and then seeing what kind of world that gives us (for the Underground Man it is not clear which is the most humiliating, to defy the laws of nature or to acknowledge them, to abide by the ideals of the culture or to flout them). The question is, what do we lose—what do we have to ignore or disown—if we use the various determinisms of science to describe what a life is? We can value scientific criteria of validity without using them to exclude other criteria. It is common knowledge—indeed, a cliché rediscovered by every child growing up—that much of what matters to us most is not necessarily convincing to other people, let alone verifiable or falsifiable.

"It is absurd," Wittgenstein writes in his "Lecture on Ethics," "to say 'Science has proved that there are no miracles.' The truth is that the scientific way of looking at a fact is not the way to look at it as a miracle." It's not that after science there are no miracles but that science might not be the best way to look at (or for) miracles. If we only look at the world scientifically, miracles become invisible. If we decided that from now on chess pieces could only be used to play checkers with, what would the word "chess" refer to? Chess would lose its grip on our imaginations, as if by magic. It would seem like a vestige of something—quaintly old-fashioned—as certain versions of ourselves begin to look after the advent of science. It was Freud's ambition that psychoanalysis should become a science, with all the prestige and cultural authority that entailed. But the dreamer and the child, as he described them, kept reminding him that there were other ways of doing things. In Freud's allegory the modern individual is the site for this conflict between the dreamer and the scientist, between the child and the realist, between the beast and the nursery.

It is perhaps worth wondering what psychoanalytic—or any other—theory would be like if it *aspired* to be more akin to children's sexual theories (and dreams, their unconscious analog) than to verifiable or falsifiable hypotheses. We could then take it for granted that psychoanalysis was a rhetoric that persuades the patient that certain ways of describing his life will improve it; that being psychoanalyzed, whatever else it is, is learning a language which, ideally, will make things better; though what those things are can only be what those languages make available. No version of psychoanalysis could then be deeper or truer than any other because there would be no already shared criteria by which they could be judged. We would think of each theorist—just like Freud's sexually curious child—as telling us how they would like the world to be, how to increase pleasure and attenuate suffering, but as often putting it in the apparently more convincing version of this-is-the-way-the-world-is (psychoanalysis would not progress, it would digress). We would assume that wishing, like culture, goes all the way down, that we can never be exempt from either. Or indeed find some superordinate position outside them from which they can be judged. Psychoanalysis, in other words, would go on answering the complicated question that Freud was among the first to ask: Why is it that adults are more like children than they want to be?

There is no unconscious that one can get closer to; there are just ways of talking that make us feel more or less hopeful. The young child could not be more hopeful. But the adults are the only available guardians of that hope. And they are the ones who make up, and choose, the stories the children will be told, the stories they will make something up with, to keep themselves going.

———

In 1934 a young American doctor called Joseph Wortis went to see Freud in Vienna for a brief "didactic" analysis in order to understand something about Freud's theories at first hand. He was professionally interested in researching homosexuality, but he was also—by the same token, as it were— curious about Freud himself. Wortis went to Freud with no pressing personal problem other than his curiosity; but quite soon Freud himself became a problem for Wortis. "Freud said he did not mean to flatter me by calling me healthy," Wortis reports in the memoir he wrote of the encounter. "I was just one of those supposedly healthy people who went about without much trouble because their complexities were stored away out of reach. 'There is no reason to feel proud of it,' he said." Throughout the analysis Wortis is incisive and explicit in his criticisms of Freud and psychoanalysis, and Freud is both what he has taught us to call defensive and dauntingly assured in his analysis of the young American's skepticism. In Wortis's spirited account it is an emblematic dialogue: between youth and age, between the New World and the Old World, between pragmatism and metaphysics, between arrogant innocence and ironic authority. (" 'I think, all things considered, I had a very fortunate and sensible upbringing.' 'I am very glad to hear that,' said Freud, 'for it is certainly unusual.' ") It is clear that Freud was not shy of teaching Wortis a thing or two, and that Wortis himself found Freud's brusque charm both exhilarating and tiresome. It is, like all good double acts—and as analysis should be—conversation at an unusual pitch. Conversation in which something that can never be known is always at stake (conflict and complexity, Freud intimates, are ultimate values, not health or normality). It is as though neither of them will allow the other to get away with his assumptions. One of Wortis's assumptions is that there is nothing much wrong with him; one of Freud's assumptions is that Wortis is keeping himself a secret, that Wortis's preoccupation with health and normality is a way of misleading himself. "There were so many ways of going wrong, I said, it seemed a wonder that anybody stayed normal. 'That reminds me of the Jew who visited a hospital,' said Freud, 'and said afterwards it was a terrible world: so many people sick and only one healthy.' " Wortis assumes that not going wrong is the aim (if not the point); Freud's association is a joke in which a Jew makes a mockery of his point of view by naively privileging it. What Freud seems to be showing Wortis in these exchanges is how Wortis simplifies himself in the interests of safety (the more normal you believe yourself to be, the madder everyone else looks); how blandly reassuring his pleasures are. It is not quite that Freud wants to pathologize Wortis, but rather that he wants to persuade him of the poverty of his much-vaunted sanity. What Wortis politely accuses Freud of is making endless unfounded assertions about what was going on inside him. The argument is about what Wortis is really like, and about what it is for anybody to be really like anything. Like all analyses it is alternatively a clash and a collaboration of vocabularies—various stories struggling for survival, various preferences becoming more or less shrill when persuasion begins to falter.

But it is in one of their early conversations that Freud is at his most stunningly deadpan. "I proceeded," Wortis writes, "to give an account of my vicissitudes in love and life. Freud made friendly and sympathetic remarks here and there, seemed to think I was well trained in honesty, and said it was . . . a good preparation for analysis. I said I was not overmuch interested in myself, and felt better when I simply went about my work. 'That is of interest, too,' said Freud. 'You have made everything you said up to now so clear it has not interested me either.' "

The abruptness of this, of course, shocks Wortis, who refers to Freud's undoing of his story two sessions later. "Freud explained that he had not meant he was uninterested, but that he thought I was, because I kept speaking of clear, superficial things." Despite Freud's disingenuousness here—or his rhetorical subtlety, depending on one's point of view—Freud nevertheless insists that clarity is trivial (that is, defensive in essence) and that being interested—having one's attention engaged—is one criterion of truthfulness. Freud assumes, in other words, that what matters is by definition interesting. But if clarity is superficial, what, in this geology of the self, is deep? And when we are not of interest to ourselves or to others, what are we up to?

To be suspicious of clarity and to value what catches our attention, to find the plausible always slightly absurd, and to be in awe of the passions— this, more or less, was what Freud wanted to impress upon Wortis. And it is of course also a description of the child, for whom indifference is never an option. If the child, and stories about childhood like psychoanalysis, have acquired a quasi-religious significance, have become our most convincing essentialism, it is perhaps because children are, as their parents always say, impossible. They want more than they can have. And, at least to begin with, they are shameless about it.

Notes

1. Omnipotence, in a psychoanalytic context, refers to the way the infant lives as though he controls the people and things that he needs; to have a wish is to assume its gratification. In fantasy—in his mind, as it were—he can have what he wants the way he wants it. The infantile part of the adult mind goes on living from this drastically hopeful perspective throughout life.

2. Sublimation, originally a term from chemistry, was a process of transformation: "The physical action or process of subliming or converting a solid substance by means of heat into vapour, which resolidifies on cooling" (O.E.D.). Freud used this analogy to describe the translation of infantile sexuality—redirection, displacement, channeling, transformation, would be some of the terms in this tricky parallel—into more socially acceptable forms of behavior. Work had to be done on the forbidden desires—a work akin to alchemy—to make them culturally viable. From a psychoanalytic point of view, sexual and aggres-

sive desires inform all cultural production, but the desires themselves are concealed. Exactly how this works—the ways in which the word is used—has always been perplexing.

3. See "The Mirror Stage as Formative of the Function of the I," in *Écrits,* by Jacques Lacan (W. W. Norton, New York, 1977); and *Therapeutic Consultations in Child Psychiatry,* by D. W. Winnicott (Basic Books, New York, 1971).

4. The apparent oxymoron "dreamwork" refers to the process of transformation that Freud said went into the making of a dream. Woven out of unconscious desire and present circumstance—what Freud called "day residues"—it was as though the dreamer had certain quasi-artistic "techniques" available to produce this unusual object: condensation, displacement, secondary revision, consideration of representability. All of this work was deemed to be in the service of making the dream sufficiently acceptable—undisturbing—to sustain the dreamer's sleep. Chapter 7 of Freud's *Interpretation of Dreams* is the original account; *Being a Character,* by Christopher Bollas (Hill & Wang, New York, 1992) is the most illuminating contemporary account. *The Innocence of Dreams,* by

Charles Rycroft (Pantheon, New York, 1979), is instructive.

In Winnicott's developmental schema the child's project is to get to what he calls "object-usage," a relationship with the mother (initially) as a real, other person. The mother becomes real when the child can acknowledge that she is not under his magical (omnipotent) control; emerging as an independent agent, the mother is depended on, not merely manipulated by the child's need. For the mother to become this real rather than exclusively imaginary object, she has to, in Winnicott's view, "survive" the child's most passionate loving and hating of her. The mother's, and therefore the child's, separateness are established by her refusing to be absolutely dominated and therefore destroyed by him. For Winnicott the child's necessary question is, how can he find something other than himself—a source outside his own imagination—to sustain him? For Winnicott's use of his concept of object-usage, see D. W. Winnicott, "The Use of an Object and Relating Through Identifications," in *Playing and Reality* (Routledge, Chapman & Hall, New York, 1982), and my "On Risk and Solitude," in *On*

Kissing, Tickling, and Being Bored (Harvard University Press, Cambridge, 1993). For the perils of dependence and much else, see Harold Boris, *Envy* (Aronson, Northvale, N.J., 1995).

5. Winnicott used the traditional squiggle game—as described in his *Therapeutic Consultations in Child Psychiatry* (see n. 3)—as a therapeutic technique in child therapy. The game involves the therapist making a squiggle on a piece of paper—an unrecognizable mark—and inviting the child to turn it into a recognizable object. Linked to Winnicott's preoccupation with what the child could make or do with what he found, he would leave spatulas on his desk when interviewing mothers and young children, noting what, if anything, the child did with these objects. From a very simple observing of this process Winnicott drew some remarkable and far-reaching conclusions about children's emotional development. See "The Observation of Infants in a Set Situation," in D. W. Winnicott, *Through Paediatrics to Psychoanalysis* (Basic Books, New York, 1974).

Bibliography

AUDEN, W. H. "Educational Theory." In *The English Auden*. Edited by Edward Mendelson. Faber, & Faber New York, 1988.

BACON, FRANCIS. Quoted in *Bacon: Portraits and Self-Portraits*. Introduction by Milan Kundera. Thames & Hudson, London, 1996.

BLAKE, WILLIAM. *The Letters of William Blake*. Edited by Geoffrey Keynes. Oxford University Press, New York, 1980.

BOUWSMA, O. K. *Wittgenstein: Conversations 1949–51*. Hackett, Indianapolis, 1986.

BROWN, NORMAN O. *Life Against Death*. Wesleyan University Press, Middletown, Conn., 1959.

DOSTOEVSKY, FYODOR. *Notes from Underground*. Translated by Richard Pevear and Larissa Volokhonsky. Vintage, New York, 1994.

ELSHTAIN, JEAN BETHKE. "The Risks and Responsibilities of Affirming Ordinary Life." In *Philosophy in an Age of Pluralism: The Philosophy of Charles Taylor in*

Question. Edited by James Tully. Cambridge University Press, New York, 1994.

EMPSON, WILLIAM. *Collected Poems.* Harcourt Brace Jovanovich, New York, 1984.

FREUD, ANNA. "The Nursery School of the Hampstead Child-Therapy Clinic." *Bulletin of the Anna Freud Centre* 11, pt. 4 (1988): 265–70.

FREUD, ANNA, AND DOROTHY BURLINGHAM. *Infants Without Families.* International Universities Press, Madison, Conn., 1943.

FREUD, SIGMUND. *The Standard Edition of the Complete Psychological Works of Sigmund Freud.* 24 vols. Translated under the general editorship of James Strachey, in collaboration with Anna Freud. W. W. Norton, New York, 1976.

FRYE, NORTHROP. *Fearful Symmetry.* Princeton University Press, Princeton, 1947.

GIDDENS, ANTHONY. *In Defense of Sociology.* Polity Press, London, 1996.

GRAHAM, W. S. *Collected Poems.* Faber & Faber, London, 1979.

Bibliography

GREEN, ANDRÉ. *On Private Madness.* International Universities Press, Madison, Conn., 1987.

HEANEY, SEAMUS. *Preoccupations.* Farrar, Straus & Giroux, 1981.

HUGHES, TED. Interview in *Paris Review* 134 (Spring 1995).

JAMES, HENRY. *The Complete Notebooks of Henry James.* Edited by Leon Edel. Oxford University Press, New York, 1987.

―――. "The Art of Fiction," In *Henry James: Essays, American and English Writers.* Edited by Leon Edel. Library of America, New York, 1984.

―――. *Letters.* Edited by Leon Edel. Harvard University Press, Cambridge, 1984.

―――. *The Wings of the Dove.* Edited by Peter Brooks. Oxford University Press, New York, 1984.

JAMES, WILLIAM. *The Principles of Psychology.* Dover, New York, 1950.

JONES, ERNEST. *Hamlet and Oedipus.* W. W. Norton, New York, 1976.

Bibliography

KAPLAN, DONALD M. *Clinical and Social Realities.* Aronson, Northvale, N.J., 1996.

KEATS, JOHN. *Letters of John Keats.* Edited by Robert Gittings. Oxford University Press, New York, 1970.

KLEIN, MELANIE. *Narrative of a Child Analysis.* Delacorte Press, New York, 1976.

LAPLANCHE, JEAN. "Psychoanalysis as Anti-hermeneutics." Translated by Luke Thurston. *Radical Philosophy* 79 (Sept.–Oct.) 1996.

LOEWALD, HANS. *Sublimation.* Yale University Press, New Haven, 1988.

MILNER, MARION. *On Not Being Able to Paint.* International Universities Press, Madison, Conn., 1990.

NEWLYN, LUCY. *Paradise Lost and the Romantic Reader.* Oxford University Press, New York, 1993.

NIETZSCHE, FRIEDRICH. *The Will to Power.* Edited by Walter Kaufman. Vintage, New York, 1968.

PONTALIS, J. B. *Love of Beginnings.* Translated by James Greene and Marie-Christine Reguis. Columbia University Press, New York, 1993.

Bibliography

RIEFF, PHILIP. *The Triumph of the Therapeutic.* Chicago University Press, Chicago, 1978.

SEGAL, HANNA. *Psychoanalysis, Literature, and War: Papers 1972–1995.* Routledge, New York, 1997.

WINNICOTT, D. W. *Thinking About Children.* Addison-Wesley, Reading, Mass., 1996.

WITTGENSTEIN, LUDWIG. "Lecture on Ethics." In *Ludwig Wittgenstein: Philosophical Occasions 1912–1951.* Hackett, Indianapolis, 1993.

WORTIS, JOSEPH. *Fragments of an Analysis with Freud.* Charter Books, New York, 1963.

Printed in the United States
by Baker & Taylor Publisher Services